D0592547

JUN — 2003

Marvin Gaye
My Brother

Marvin Gaye
My Brother

by Frankie Gaye

with Fred E. Basten

Backbeat
Books

San Francisco

Published by Backbeat Books
600 Harrison Street, San Francisco, CA 94107
www.backbeatbooks.com
email: books@musicplayer.com

CMP
United Business Media

An imprint of the Music Player Group
Publishers of *Guitar Player, Bass Player, Keyboard,* and other magazines
United Entertainment Media, Inc.
A CMP Information company

Distributed to the book trade in the US and Canada by
Publishers Group West, 1700 Fourth Street, Berkeley, CA 94710

Distributed to the music trade in the US and Canada by
Hal Leonard Publishing, P.O. Box 13819, Milwaukee, WI 53213

Text Design and Composition by Leigh McLellan
Cover Design by Richard Leeds - bigwigdesign.com
Front Cover Photo: Michael Ochs Archives.com
Back Cover Photo: Gaye Family Archives

All interior photos are courtesy of the Gaye Family Archives

Library of Congress Cataloging-in-Publication Data

Gaye, Frankie, 1941-2001
    Marvin Gaye, my brother / by Frankie Gaye with Fred E. Basten
        p. cm.
    Includes index.
    ISBN 0-87930-742-0 (alk. paper)
Gaye, Marvin. 2. Singers—United States—Biography.
I. Basten Fred E. II. Title.

ML420.G305G39 2003
782.421644'092—dc21
[B]   2003040422

Printed in the United States of America

03 04 05 06 07   5 4 3 2 1

Contents

Introduction

On the evening of January 23, 2002, the A&E cable television station premiered an hour-long biography of Marvin Gaye. Many of Marvin's friends and coworkers were interviewed on camera, along with his sisters, Jeanne and Zeola ("Sweetsie"), and his brother Frankie. Everyone had personal remembrances to tell along the way; everyone, that is, except Frankie. He smiled his way through most of his interview without revealing too much, but he looked as if he had a whole lot more to say. He certainly did.

There was a reason for Frankie's silence. At the time of the taping, he was finishing his own biography of Marvin, a very personal story of two brothers and their most unusual journey together through life.

Marvin and Frankie were as close as brothers could be. Only a few years apart in age—Marvin was two-and-a-half years older—they were almost identical in appearance, especially as they grew into their teens. They told each other everything; they knew each other's secrets. They knew so much about each other that Frankie became the prime target for information following Marvin's sudden, headline-making death in 1984, on the eve of his forty-fifth birthday. As much as Frankie liked to talk, he rarely said yes to callers wanting to know about his famous brother and his father. He saw a handful of them, but he said little or nothing, keeping the important information and best stories to himself. He asked the same of many people who had known or worked with Marvin. "Save it for me," he told them. "Save it for my book."

So much has been written about Marvin in the years since his death, and much of it upset Frankie. "Those people never told the whole story, how or why things happened, or what *really* happened," he has said. "To know Marvin's life, you have to understand the atmosphere that created Marvin Gaye."

Frankie was especially sensitive about falsehoods that had been reported about his family. But he kept quiet, knowing that one day the truth would be told. It was Frankie's dream to tell the story himself, but he refused to commit a word to paper while his father was still alive. Even after all that had happened, he did not want to hurt his father.

Marvin Pentz Gay, Sr., died October 18, 1998. Several months later I received a call from Wallace Peoples, a friend of Frankie's and mine. "Would you be interested in working with Frankie Gaye on a book of remembrances about his brother Marvin?" he asked. I couldn't say no.

Wallace brought Frankie over to my place for a quick meeting, then a week later we got together for lunch at a restaurant in Santa Monica. We clicked from the start, but getting together after that wasn't easy. As much as Frankie wanted to start working on his book, he first had to take care of other commitments.

After Marvin's death, Frankie's own career as a singer and songwriter began to take off. He was much in demand in clubs, particularly in England and Canada, as well as in various cities in the United States. He recorded a tribute song to Marvin called "My Brother," which made the charts in Great Britain. He also released an album called *The Very Best of Frankie Gaye,* and he had dates for appearances in Pittsburgh, New York, and Detroit, where he and Kim Weston recorded TV promotional spots singing "It Takes Two," a song Weston had recorded with Marvin in 1966. The two were accompanied by former members of the Funk Brothers, Motown's backup group.

Over two months passed before Frankie was finally able to settle down and meet with me on a regular basis. At first it wasn't easy for Frankie to let his thoughts out; he was hesitant to open up, knowing his thoughts were being recorded. But he began to relax, and once he started talking it was hard to keep him quiet. Reaching so deep into his memory, though, and talking about subjects that he'd tried so hard to suppress for years, was painful for him. Most of the time, however, his face would brighten with joy as he recalled the good times. Like Marvin, Frankie could hold an audience with his singing. Had he not devoted his life to music and to Marvin's career, he could have made a living entertaining crowds as a speaker. He was a born storyteller.

Our sessions together—twice a week for a little over a year— were captured on scores of tapes. I also collected reams of notes from our numerous telephone conversations between meetings.

With all the information at hand, Frankie and I began writing the book. We were making steady progress when he was called to appear for the taping of a segment about Marvin Gaye on A&E's *Biography* series; the segment was scheduled to air in late January 2002. As excited as he was about his book, he purposely avoided mention of it during his on-camera interview. In fact, he said as little as he could about Marvin, wanting his book to say it all.

In mid-December, only weeks after the *Biography* taping, Frankie suddenly became ill and was rushed to a nearby hospital in Santa Monica. Two days later, he was gone, due to a heart attack.

"Frankie Gaye, Marvin's younger brother, passed away over the holidays," announced *Biography* host Harry Smith as the program came to a close. "Frankie was one of the last people who could have set the record straight on his celebrated sibling. Now that he too is gone, one can't help but wonder if the truth behind the talent and torment that was Marvin Gaye will ever be told."

Although Frankie would not see the publication of this book, he left knowing that it would be published—and the truth would finally be told.

Fred E. Basten

1

It was Sunday, April 1st, 1984, the day before my brother, Marvin Gaye's forty-fifth birthday. The morning had started quietly, so relaxed that I hadn't bothered to put on anything more than my sweat suit. My wife, Irene, was in the kitchen fixing our breakfast, while our fourteen-month-old daughter, April, was asleep in her room. I was waiting to tape one of my favorite movies, *Shane.* I had seen the film a dozen or more times, knew every scene and line by heart. Even so, I looked forward to seeing it again and taping it for my growing video library. But I had more on my mind than the movie or Marvin's birthday. The way things were going, tomorrow would not be a day for celebration.

I hadn't seen Marvin yet, but Irene had. She had gone to the big house next door to take Mother her breakfast, but Mother wasn't ready to eat yet, so she asked Irene to take the tray into Marvin's room. He looked bad, Irene said, and he had a hard time sitting up in bed. His muscles ached, he told her. Other than that, Irene reported, the house was calm, which was a good way to start the day.

It wasn't always calm next door. Lately, it had been a madhouse over there. Lots of arguing—yelling and screaming going on between

Marvin and Father. Marvin was in bad shape; Father wasn't doing too well, either.

As I waited for the movie to start, I was also expecting a call from Dave Simmons, Marvin's close friend and mine. Dave knew what was going on in the big house. I didn't have to tell him; he had seen for himself. The time had come, we both agreed, to get help for Marvin. We were going to get him out of the house and into psychiatric care. We couldn't wait any longer. Maybe we had waited too long already.

Five months earlier, following the end of Marvin's United States tour, he had moved into the two-story English Tudor–style house on Gramercy Place, in Los Angeles, to be with Mother. She had still not fully recovered from a serious operation. In times of trouble, Marvin always came home. Home was his refuge.

Marvin had begun to act strangely during the tour. He was heavily on drugs, but that was nothing new. It was the death threats he had received—or believed he had received. No one knew if they were real or imagined, but in Marvin's mind they were real. Dave Simmons and I suspected they weren't real, but we shadowed his every move, just in case. He also insisted on having bodyguards nearby while he was onstage—and everywhere else he went. Even with protection, he grew more fearful as the weeks passed.

At home, Marvin's problems escalated, along with his paranoia and drug use. Physically and mentally, he was a mess. He became convinced that nobody loved him. It hurt even more to hear him say that he trusted no one.

Mother didn't know what to do. Father simply tried to stay out of Marvin's way, often closing himself in his own bedroom down the hall. Staying out of the way wasn't always possible. For most of Marvin's life, he and Father had been at odds. Their arguments had become more frequent and heated since Marvin's return home.

A little after eleven o'clock on that Sunday morning, April 1st, as I was watching television and waiting for the phone to ring, Irene said she heard a shot from outside. I thought I'd heard a car backfire, nothing more. Then I heard another bang, and another. Irene came running in from the kitchen. We both got frightened when we heard Mother screaming outside. I went for my shoes as Irene hurried outside. She was holding Mother in her arms when I reached them. "He's shot Marvin," she sobbed. "He's killed my boy."

I was inside the front door before I heard the last of Mother's words, but I'd heard enough. Father had shot Marvin, and I had to get to him.

The house was quiet and dark; the shades had been drawn to keep out the strong morning sunlight. I stood in the entryway for a second or two trying to unscramble my thoughts. Turning on a light never occurred to me.

My first concern was for Marvin. I had to find him, but where was he? And where was Father? Did he still have a gun? And in what frame of mind would I find him? I didn't even know if Father had really shot Marvin. Maybe Mother had imagined that, just as Marvin had probably imagined he was being stalked. But we'd heard the gunshots. What was going on in this crazy house? I didn't have time to think about it. I had to find out what had really happened; I had to find Marvin.

Cautiously, I walked down the hallway to the back stairs that led to Marvin's room on the second floor. It was so quiet that all I could hear was the sound of my own breathing. With each step the pounding in my chest grew stronger.

My mind began to play tricks on me. For brief flashes, I began to feel that I was back in the jungles of Vietnam. Slowly moving forward, it was impossible to know what, or who, I would find behind the next giant leaf or tree trunk. But I was in my parents' home, and somewhere in the dim light ahead, if Mother's words were true, my brother lay bleeding, maybe dying, maybe dead.

I began to say Marvin's name, softly at first, then louder. "Marvin, Marvin," I cried. "Marvin, where are you? Answer me, Marvin." There was nothing but silence. I called again. "Marvin ... Marvin ...."

2

"*M*arvin, where are you? Answer me, Marvin!"

It was Father's voice. He was standing in the doorway to our home in Simple City, the lowest slum in all of Washington, D.C. As children, Marvin and I were never allowed to wander out of earshot. Father always had to know where we were; he kept close tabs on us.

"Marvin! Marvin!"

I can still hear his voice calling.

Father was a tough disciplinarian, but in his way, he was fair. He was simply trying to teach us right from wrong, and that wasn't always easy where we lived. Besides, it was impossible to argue with the Word of God, and everything Father believed stemmed from the Bible. In Simple City, he was minister at the House of God, a struggling, one-room storefront church with a tiny, three-family congregation.

Father was born in 1914, in Lexington, Kentucky, and raised on religion by his mother, Mamie, who was the first woman to become a member of the Pentecostal House of God. One of 18 children, Father started going to church as a child, and he spent the next 40 years evangelizing.

It was during one of his road trips, in 1934, traveling with Sister Fame, that he met our Mother, Alberta, who was also Southern born. Father was a handsome twenty-year-old when he caught Mother's eye. They were married in 1935, in Washington, D.C. Mother already had a child, Michael, but Father made it clear he had no interest in raising another man's son. Young Michael was handed over to one of Mother's sisters, Pearl, and it wasn't until Michael was in his teens that he learned the identity of his real mother.

There were other family secrets. Mother's father died in the insane asylum to which he had been committed after he had shot and wounded our grandmother. Members of Father's family, too, were always in trouble, and again, guns were involved. I've heard tales of bloodshed and murder running through the family tree. But even more hush-hush were the identities of Father's brothers—five in all—who were said to have been homosexual, which was a terrible stigma for a family to bear at that time, especially a black family growing up in a Southern ghetto.

Some people wondered about our Father, too. Marvin and I were often told as children that Father acted effeminate, only some would come right out and say, "Your papa's a sissy." We would stick up for Father, of course, because we wanted to prove we weren't sissies too. That wasn't always easy. Although Motown later changed Marvin's name to "Gaye," we grew up with the name "Gay"; we learned early on that Gay was "a bad word," so we were constantly being teased about that, too. At one point the teasing became so intense that we had to take secret routes to and from school to avoid bumping into the other kids. Seems like Marvin and me spent half of our lives running.

Our two sisters—older sister, Jeanne, and baby sister, Zeola, who we called "Sweetsie"—didn't get as much razzing as we did. Being a "Gay" and being a girl seemed to be okay in those days. Or maybe boys were just more sensitive to name-calling.

Our family name was originally "Gaylord." When the "lord" was dropped, no one knows, but Marvin would say, "I'd rather be called Marvin Lord."

"Gay means happiness," Father told him.

"No, it don't," replied Marvin.

I had a hard time with my first name, too. It's really Frances, a unisex name. So early on I didn't have just one name to fight over, I had two. My parents decided to give in and call me Frankie. Then I couldn't wait for the movie "Frankie and Johnnie" to come out. But guess what—Frankie was—a *girl!*

Since Marvin was named after Father, his middle name was also "Pentz," a name black people don't know about. Marvin got teased about that, too, and he hated it. It was hard to spell and he couldn't explain it. There was a lot of stuttering going on in school when Marvin was asked his middle name. He'd go, "Wha ... wha ... what did you say?" The name is actually white—not white American but white European. It was derived from the coin, pence.

As a youngster, sister Zeola had a problem with her name. She would be asked, "Isn't that the plane that dropped the atom bomb on Japan?" That was Enola Gay, not Zeola Gay. She could never tell her name to a Japanese person without getting a strange look. What were our parents thinking about when they named us?

Me and Marvin felt we had three strikes against us from the start. Our name was one strike, but we had to live with that. We also had to live with being black, which affected us most when we traveled outside of Simple City. But the biggest strike of all was Father's religion. It was his life, so it became our life.

As kids, it was difficult for us to separate Father's religious world from the real world. We were Seventh Day Adventists, which was a bizarre mixture of Orthodox Judaism and Pentecostal Christianity. "The Sabbath was strange," Marvin once said, "because things stopped for us every Friday night at sundown." It was true. We couldn't play, we couldn't do anything except pray and praise God. Saturdays were spent in church since, according to the Bible (and Father), Saturday was the seventh day, a day of rest and prayer. While we were in church, other kids were outside playing. On Sundays, when everyone else was in church clothes, we were in our hand-me-downs. Neighbors stared and passed us by.

When kids asked, "Why don't you go to church on Sunday?" the Gay kids would reply, "Because God didn't rest on the first day. Anybody who can count knows that!" And they would say, "You're crazy!" Me and Marvin would then tell them, "You can say anything you want," to which the other kids would answer, "We don't want to talk to you anymore." We were the number-one strange family around.

The only drawback to our religion for Father, was employment. In those days, everyone worked a six-day week, so no one would hire Father because he couldn't work on Saturdays. It didn't matter that he could work on Sundays. No one worked on Sundays. And since we couldn't live on the tithes from Father's little church, it was left to Mother to mainly support the family as a domestic. Down deep, however, Father always believed that "God will provide."

That was inspiring but not always true. One Thanksgiving, we were so poor that Mother had to make soup for dinner. The soup was delicious, but it had no turkey in it, so all of us kids complained. "You're eating, aren't you?" Father said with a glare. Then he launched into the story about the child with no shoes and the man with no feet.

The best part of church for us was the music, the rollicking, joyous, hand-clapping songs. We had an old secondhand piano at home, and Marvin wanted to learn how to play. A friend of Mother's volunteered to give him lessons, but she didn't have the patience to work with him. Marvin wanted to move along faster. She tried to slow him down, but she couldn't, so she had to step aside. That's when Father took over and taught Marvin how to play the piano. Seeing Marvin and Father working so well together gave us all hope. That was the happiest I ever saw the two of them together.

With Father's help, Marvin took to the piano quickly; he loved music, and he told Father so. "So does God," Father reminded him.

"It says in the Bible to make a joyful sound." Before too long, Marvin was playing piano in church.

A requirement of Father's church was to have a church activity. Ours was singing. "That's the only way to go," said Marvin. "Heck with learning all the Scriptures."

Marvin had always liked to sing, but he never had the nerve to sing in front of anyone except at home, and then only sheepishly. In church, however, he started singing with the tiny choir. Then, one Saturday, he got up and sang "His Eye Is on the Sparrow," with Father backing him on the piano. It was quiet as everyone listened, and when he finished he heard the applause and felt the hugs. It was the most attention he had ever received. Until that moment in church, Marvin really never knew he could sing or affect other people with his voice.

In 1950, when Marvin was eleven, we appeared on a stage together for the first time. We were doing a musical play at Children's Theater, a little run-down building at a local playground. Marvin sang "Be My Love," a song made popular that year by Mario Lanza in the movie *The Toast of New Orleans*. That was a real turning point for Marvin, and it was almost impossible to keep him quiet after that.

With Father home so much, it wasn't easy to have fun. Of course, we were never allowed to play inside the house, so that left the immediate outside, which wasn't the greatest place to play. Being kids, we were often tempted to wander off, and that's when we'd hear father calling out our names. We were certain he lived at the front window whenever we went outside. Things got better when Beatrice Carson came to live with us. Dear Bea. She was a distant cousin of Mother's, and just to make certain we got the relationship straight, she'd remind us that we were related "in a marriage way."

Bea was like a big sister to Mother, and she was a big help around the house. Mother worked so hard cleaning people's houses; before Bea came, she never got any rest, even when she came home. With Bea there Mother could relax a little. Bea cleaned, cooked for us, even took us out on the town. "On weekends," Bea remembers, "little Marvin and Frankie always wanted to go 'bye-bye.' Marvin was six then and Frankie was about four, so I'd get them ready and we'd ride the trolley to the end of the line, then ride back. There was a canal along the way, and they could look out into the water. Other times we'd take the bus and ride around for free with a pass. The kids had fun."

Having Bea with us made it easier to stray when Father left the house, and as we got older we strayed farther away. On hot summer days we'd wander off to the swimming hole. It was the only place to cool off that was closer than the Atlantic Ocean, but it belonged to the Potomac Electric Company, and it was fenced in with a big "No Trespassing" sign. I'm sure there was a sign that said "Danger," too, because there was a suction pump that made swimming hazardous. But nothing could stop Marvin, me, or any of the other local kids from crawling under the fence for a dip. As the youngest, I was always the first to jump in—I had to, I was the guinea pig— then the others would follow. One day, one of the kids got too close to the pump and drowned. That was a huge tragedy in the neighborhood, and after that, Father was even more strict with us. He wouldn't let Marvin or me out of his sight.

How Marvin looked forward to the days when Father was away. He was always looking for new ways to get in trouble, and somehow it always involved me. He'd found a tree in a vacant area and decided it was perfect for playing "parachute jump." With Father's umbrella in hand, he led me to the tree and told me to climb up and jump. "It's fun," he said. "The umbrella will catch the air and you'll float down." I jumped and fell to the ground in a heap. Marvin just looked down at his little brother and said, "Hmmmmm, I thought it would hold you." From then on Father made us stay indoors when he was gone, saying, "Freedom don't mean doing what you want to do. You always have to follow rules. There's no place you can go without rules, except Heaven."

Marvin always had to think everything out. If it didn't make sense to him, he wouldn't go for it. He was so full of questions, and he kept trying to come up with one that would stump Father. One day he asked, "Who were God's mother and father?"

"Some things you leave alone," Father replied. And that was the end of that.

Marvin had an opinion on just about everything. He would start off by saying, "I think ..." and Father would cut him off with, "It's not what you think but what you say, so keep your mouth shut."

"I can breathe, can't I?" Marvin would answer.

Marvin had some snappy comebacks, but Father would have none of his sass. "As Jesus said," he would tell him, " 'It would be better that you cut your tongue from your mouth and live your life.' The tongue is the gateway to hell. People say the wrong things with it. They eat the wrong things with it. The tongue is the enemy of the body."

We had so many rules to live by. For instance, women couldn't wear sleeveless dresses, even in the heat of summer. They couldn't wear nylons, lipstick, or nail polish, or show their hair or wear open-toed shoes. Mother didn't mind, but older sister Jeanne wasn't too happy about the restrictions. All the fun things, such as dancing, movies, and television, were out for us. And we had a restricted diet. No pork products.

Mother was the greatest cook. She could cook anything and you'd swear it was the best you'd ever eaten. That's why she was often hired for parties given by doctors and lawyers at the best houses in the suburbs. It was always a treat for Mother when the family was invited to a friend's house for dinner, because it got her out of the kitchen. One evening we arrived to hear, "We have a surprise for you ... a big pot of chitlins!" Everyone in the ghetto eats ribs, chitlins, pigs' feet and hog's head. They taste so good you want to smack your grandmother. So Marvin and I were jumping up and down yelling, "Ooooo, chitlins! Chitlins! Chitlins!" But we couldn't eat chitlins, and we knew it. We were just putting on a show because our friends thought they had prepared something special for us. As Father was about to let the word out, Marvin, genius that he was, bent over as if he had a sudden pain.

Father was used to Marvin's pranks, so he pretended to take him seriously. "What's wrong, son?" he asked. Then he grabbed Marvin and said, "Oh, no, it's his appendix flaring up again. We'd better take him to the hospital. And just as I'm about to eat chitlins!" Once outside and in the car, Father turned to us and said, "Whew, that was a close one."

So many rules to follow. As kids, we were often angry thinking about what Father and Mother had gotten us into. Being older than I was, Marvin was more adventurous. Early on I learned from Marvin's mistakes, mistakes that led to spankings, or what we'd call "whippins." I'd see what Marvin was doing and tell myself, "So that's what happens when you get caught." Even so, I had my own share of whippings, plenty of them, mostly because of Marvin. Not always, but mostly.

Various incidents remain in my memory, among them the time Father thought I had stolen a bicycle. Then there was the night Marvin had eaten the choicest pieces of fried chicken that Mother had prepared for the next day's company. So he wouldn't get blamed, Marvin smeared chicken grease around my mouth as I slept, then put the bones under my bed. I got the blame, and another whipping.

We weren't really bad kids—we couldn't be, with Father around so much and with all his teaching. We learned early on never to hit anyone. Hitting was not a good thing to do. Worst of all would be to hit your parents. Father would tell us, "The Bible says, 'Honor thy father and mother that their days may be long.' "

There was another saying he was fond of telling us. It went something like: "I brought you into this world, and if you ever lay a hand on me, *I* will take you out."

I don't know about Marvin but it didn't make much of an impression on me at the time. Hitting my parents was the last thing I wanted to do. Still, I never forgot Father's words. I guess Marvin never did either.

3

As Marvin was nearing his fourteenth birthday, we were forced to move from the slum section of Washington, D.C. Our part of town had been infested with rats for years, but nothing had ever been done about it. The problem was so bad, in fact, that we had to keep a coal bucket filled with stones inside the house to throw at the rats. Lucky for us, there was more action outside than inside, especially when we went on rat hunts. Four or five of us kids would wander around throwing rocks at whatever looked like good hiding places, like garbage cans. Once we hit a garbage can and huge rats jumped out and began running in all directions. Stones flew, even at one of the big brown rodents headed Marvin's way. He ran off yelling, "Hey, don't kill me," more afraid of the rocks than the rat.

City officials basically ignored the rats until one got into a baby's crib and started eating its fingers. The cries for help from Simple City were finally heard, and local papers headlined our plight. Fearing that the rats would spread into other areas, the city took drastic action by razing our part of town. The message seemed to be that it didn't matter if *we* died as long as the rats didn't go anywhere.

Along with the other families, we were moved from the southwest section to the newly built projects on the northeast side of town, which was actually the end of the city. There were no businesses there, only people. If you wanted to go somewhere, and you didn't have a car, you had to walk almost a mile to get to a bus stop.

Despite some inconveniences, our new place on East Capitol was much nicer and way bigger. We had huge front and back yards, and even an extra room. Now the piano had its own room, and the living room was again basically off limits.

The change was heavy, like starting over. In the new house, Mother and Father, Jeanne and Sweetsie, and Marvin and I each shared bedrooms. It was at night in our beds that Marvin and I talked about music. I called him a dreamer because of his faraway look, and he would say, "Man, I hear music."

As a kid, I really didn't understand what he meant. I liked music and singing too, probably because we were so close, but it wasn't the only thing I thought about. Marvin had a one-track mind. He just loved music; he couldn't get enough of it. I guess when you have a talent that natural, and it comes so easily, you know. Marvin knew.

We talked about the kinds of music he wanted to sing, and it wasn't only spirituals. "There are so many kinds of music," he said one night, "and it's all good."

"But what about Father?"

"He loves music," Marvin answered. "He taught me all I know. When we sit down at the piano, next to each other, all is good. He'll be okay."

"I don't know about that."

"Music is the language of the world," Marvin said. "The Bible is filled with references to music."

"I know," I said, "but there's the Lord's music and there's the ..."

"I'd never sing the devil's music," he said, cutting me off. "Besides, it's not the music that gets Father, it's the words. There are ways of saying things that aren't bad. Stop worrying."

I wasn't worrying, not at that point in our lives. I was happy for Marvin. He seemed to have everything worked out, and I prayed that his dream would come true for him. Years later, as I looked back on our conversations together, I thought, be careful what you pray for.

Marvin kept singing in church and thinking of little else but music. Whenever Father was away from the house, if only briefly, Marvin would change the station on our radio from gospel to pop music, then he would clap his hands to the rhythms and sing along with the songs. He had a range that was way beyond mine, especially when he sang high notes in falsetto. His voice sounded so clear and fluid, so natural. He wanted to sing everything; he'd have sung the nightly prayer at dinner if only Father would have let him.

We each had one night a week to say a verse from the Bible at the dinner table. Sister Jeanne learned one that went on and on and on. Even Father became impatient to eat and would cut her off. "We'd like to get to the food before it goes cold, please," he told her. "Save the rest for next time."

Marvin and I had a hard time coming up with verses for our turns. The Bible was so thick with pages, and the pages were covered with all those lines to read. And some of the words were beyond us. "I don't have time," Marvin told me after only a few minutes with the Good Book, so it was left to me to come up with something to say.

I scanned the pages as best I could and finally found a verse we could memorize. It was only two words: "Jesus wept." We ran that one into the ground until Father made us come up with a more challenging passage.

Few things made Father really happy. One was keeping his family in tow. The other was looking forward to attending the annual Seventh Day Adventist Convention. He planned on going every year, but since the gathering of ministers was always held out of town, he could never afford it. Finally, after years of saving, money earned mostly by Mother, he was able to go.

The days leading up to his departure were the most peaceful the family had ever known. Father's mind was on the glorious days ahead, which he knew would be the biggest of his life—ever. It was the calling of the clan and he was happy as a lark.

He was gone less than a week when he returned. He headed straight for his room, said nothing, and we hardly saw him for days. When he finally came out for more than a few minutes, he paid no attention to any of us for the longest time. He was a different man.

Mother found out what was bothering him but she wouldn't tell us, not for a while, anyway. When she did, she spoke with a broken heart. It seems when Father arrived at the convention he saw the other ministers driving up to the hotel in new cars and wearing threads of gold with diamonds on their fingers.

Father never knew the church was rich. He had taken a vow of poverty. He had lost jobs by not being able to work on Saturday.

He sent all but the smallest portion of the money he received from his congregation to the church, and in doing so, had sacrificed for his family. "I've been true to the church," he told Mother. "How could the church do that to me?"

Father's faith in God never wavered; he loved God so much. But he had lost his faith in the church, and our churchgoing days were over. His decision to leave the church had an impact on all the family. We still believed, we still prayed, but the laws of the church were no longer held over us. From then on we were bound strictly by the Word of God, the Bible.

Marvin's head was in the clouds. His faith in Jesus and God was as strong as ever, but other sounds were buzzing loudly in his ears. At William Randall Junior High, the only subject that kept him from dreaming was music. Nothing else on this earth meant as much to him.

Marvin had made a good friend named Reese Palmer in school. Reese knew his way around the new neighborhood and knew all the guys our age, including many who also happened to love music and singing. They'd get together and sing doo wop on the corner of 60th and East Capitol Street, which wasn't too far from where we lived. I soon began tagging along and joining in.

By the time Marvin and Reese got to Cardoza High, the group was going strong, and even had a name: the D.C. Tones. Some of the group from Randall Junior High had dropped out, but replacements were always standing by. It was through Reese that we met Geraldine Adams, who liked to be called Peasie, a name given to her by her older sister Jeannette, because her growing hair came out twisted, looking like little peas.

Peasie was a sweetheart. She grew up with us, and she was always there to give us hope, love, and inspiration. Like Reese, she knew just about everyone in the neighborhood, from the friendly children and their families to the local roughnecks.

"Marvin wasn't one of the bullies in the neighborhood," Reese says. "I used to get beat up trying to look out for him. Guys were jealous 100 percent of his good looks and cool." It probably did bother some of the toughs, and every community had them, that Marvin was so easygoing and refused to fight. He couldn't, or wouldn't; Father would have been proud of him.

Many of the project kids who couldn't sing were simply jealous. Says Peasie, "If you could sing or if you were in the know with somebody, you could hang out with us. But if you couldn't sing or dance, you had to stay home."

Marvin always said that singing with the D.C. Tones was great training in harmonizing for him, and exposed him to a range of contemporary music and sounds. He sure spent more time singing than thinking about his schoolwork. "Throughout all of high school," says Reese, "Marvin and I hung out in the hallways and bathrooms, singing instead of going to class, which was strange because we never got caught. Marvin already knew just about everything they were trying to teach us, and most of what I knew I learned from him. A lot of people, including his father, accused me of leading him to where he shouldn't go, but it was just the opposite."

The D.C. Tones sprang into song at every possible chance. It didn't matter if they stood on a street corner, a neighbor's doorstep, a front porch, in an alleyway—or if they really didn't have a sound of their own. It was just fine to be compared to the smooth blendings of the Drifters, the Platters, even the Orioles.

No matter how much fun the D.C. Tones had singing, and counting the coins that had been thrown into a hat by the folks who had gathered around, Marvin and I always had to be home by sundown. Even though we were older, Father still had to know our whereabouts, which meant we had to be within earshot. The guys in the group got on us for that. "Your papa is calling," they would taunt, and they would mimic his voice. Those rare times when he didn't yell for us, we still knew when the moment had come to leave, or we'd hear about it when we got home. The neighborhood parents loved us because we were so obedient, but that didn't sit well with the other kids our age. "Don't go," they'd say, "stick around, stay."

"Can't," Marvin would answer.

"You're breakin' us up too early."

"You know how it is. We have to get home."

Then they'd snarl at us. "Why do you always have to be so good?"

"Never mind," he'd reply. Then we'd be off, telling ourselves, "Oh, Lord, we'll probably get beat up tomorrow."

An added advantage to singing with the group was girls. We'd see them coming, sing louder, and give our bodies an extra wiggle. They'd walk by and act flirty, then giggle. We knew we could have any girl we wanted. That didn't necessarily mean we knew what to do with them or that we'd stop boasting that we had 'gone all the way.'" Actually, it would be quite some time before either Marvin or I could say those words and not be lying.

Singing had been therapy for Marvin. For someone so basically shy, he loved the attention that street-singing brought him. But street-singing was different than singing in church, where he had to stand alone in front of people. Solo singing made him nervous, but being one of a group gave him a feeling of security. At school he was on his own, too; he alone was responsible for his grades. Not being a good reader made studying difficult, and most subjects bored him, which is part of why he went to class as little as possible. History and geography weren't nearly as much fun as music. Not being a good student, or even a fair one, created problems at home. Marvin was always having to explain his poor grades to Father. Something had always come between them to create trouble, and his performance at school added to the tension.

Marvin was barely seventeen when he made a surprise announcement: he had enlisted in the Air Force. He had wanted to leave school for a long time, and what better way to get out of school, and away from Father and D.C., than to sign up? Father nearly had a fit. "You in the Air Force? That's a laugh," he said, glaring at his namesake. "You'll never make the grade."

"I will," Marvin answered. "Why do you say I won't?" He was in for another lecture, and he knew it.

"Because you're not tough enough. You can't take criticism."

"I can do it," said Marvin, "and I will."

"You *think* you will!" Father snapped.

Marvin didn't respond. He simply kept his head down, acting like he was deep in thought. All he wanted to do was get out of the house. Instead, he went to our room. I wasn't surprised when the door opened a few minutes later and Mother walked in.

"I know why you want to go, Marvin," she said in her tender way, "but have you really thought this all out?"

"I really have, yes, Mother."

"Have you?" she pressed.

"He won't let me do anything. It's time I got off on my own, away from all this."

"You know, Marvin, there's no escaping rules. Wherever you go or however big you become, you always have to answer to somebody."

"There's got to be a place, there's got to be."

"Like I've told you before, there's only one place that I know, and that's Heaven."

"Well, I've got to see for myself," he said. "I've just got to get away. It'll all work out."

Mother forced a smile and said, "If it don't you know you can always come back." Then she wrapped him in her arms.

Before Marvin left for the Air Force, Father's parting words were, "Remember what I told you. You'll never make the grade."

Marvin didn't respond, he simply walked out the door and kept going, never looking back. He knew he was at last off on his own, certain that he'd no longer have to listen to anyone put him down. No Father, no school, no bullies. If he had thought things out, as he'd told Mother he did, he sure mustn't have spent much time doing it.

4

*F*ather was right. Marvin couldn't make it in the Air Force. His basic training at Lackland Air Force Base, in San Antonio, Texas, included courses in mechanics, electronics, and firearms, which were of zero interest to him. From there, he was transferred to Francis E. Warren Air Force Base, in Cheyenne, Wyoming, then to Schilling Air Force Base, in Salina, Kansas, for more training. "It's like I'm back in school," he said during one of his frequent calls to Mother and me, moaning and groaning all the while he talked. "And they've got me doing dumb stuff like peeling potatoes." Mother sympathized, but I could only tease him.

It wasn't long before he began rebelling. He got bad marks during his barracks' inspections, began showing up late for duty, and was caught off base one night. He wanted to get kicked out of the service, but he only got dressed-down by his commanding officer. "What else do I have to do to get sent home?" he grumbled from faraway Kansas. "It's a horror show here, the worst time of my life. I must have been plenty desperate to get into this mess."

"I still don't know why you did it," I told him, referring to his enlistment. "That was dumb."

"They said I could be in Special Services. I told them I wanted to be in shows, to do some entertaining."

"Who said that?"

"Some old guy at the sign-up office."

"That's what he said? You're sure?"

"I'm not sure of anything anymore. All I know is that's what I told the man I wanted when he asked. Who'd volunteer for this crap?"

"Well, you're stuck in it now."

"Not for long," Marvin said. "I'll figure a way to get out!" And he did. He pretended to have a nervous breakdown and began acting crazy. He defied authority by ignoring orders and regulations, no matter who issued them. An appointment with a military psychiatrist was set up, but Marvin stubbornly refused to go. His behavior finally convinced his superiors that he was not Air Force material. Marvin had enlisted in October 1956, and less than eight months later he was given a discharge "under honorable conditions." Marvin had clearly shown that he was not worth the military's time, effort, and money.

"I'm out!" he squealed over the phone, unable to wait until he got home to tell us his good news. That wasn't all; he had more to tell, but not for Mother's ears. "Guess what," he said, without pausing a beat to let me guess. "I've finally gone all the way. It happened at one of those cathouses around the base. I sneaked off and got laid." It wasn't all that great, he admitted. That was probably because he was no better a lover at that age than he was an airman trainee. But he didn't admit to that.

Mother's arms were stretched out wide to welcome Marvin home. "My boy," she said, sounding like he had just won a medal, "it's so good to have you back."

Father just stood there, staring at Mother carrying on. He had never hugged Marvin, or any of us for that matter, because as he so often pounded into us, he showed his love through his teaching and discipline. And now he had new words for Marvin, and they weren't the kind of words Marvin could embrace. They came out in a torrent, sharp and unending, as if he were delivering a sermon to fallen souls. Since Father had been proven right about Marvin's inability to succeed in the Air Force, he could not let him forget it. It was much more stinging than a simple, "I told you so."

Marvin wasn't told that he was not welcome at home, but he knew if he stayed it wouldn't be pleasant, at least not until Father calmed down. Knowing Father, that wouldn't be anytime soon.

Being a rebel, Marvin wasn't quite as afraid of Father as the rest of us, but living with his frequent outbursts did not make for a happy homecoming. He had to get away, if only temporarily, so he called around and found an open door at Peasie's, which was perfect. Her apartment was just far enough away from Father but still close to home. "We lived on the same street and I'd see Mr. and Mrs. Gay every once in a while," Peasie remembers. "They knew Marvin was staying with me so they'd tell me to take some money to Marvin. I'd get the money from Mrs. Gay and give it to Marvin so he could have a little change in his pocket now and then." Peasie knew what Marvin was going through at home. "Marvin and I had perhaps the strictest parents in the area," she says. "Marvin was a little rebellious at times. I guess I was too, because me and my father never got along. Kids can go a little too far and the parents have to say, 'Okay, we're in control.' Basically, Mr. Gay was not a mean man, not a bad man at all. He was just trying to teach the kids properly."

Living in the apartment below Peasie was another good friend of Marvin's, Reese Palmer. During Marvin's brief stint in the Air Force, several changes had taken place. Peasie, who was several years older than Marvin, had gotten married, and Reese had graduated from Cardoza High School. Now, with only small change in his pockets, Marvin was looking for work. So was Reese. They found jobs working in the Hot Shop Commissary, which was basically a food warehouse in northwest D.C. "They had us working on the inside filling orders for the different Howard Johnson coffee shops," remembers

Reese. "We'd be in the icebox with big jackets on or standing by the door of the freezer. No matter where we were working, we were always singing. One day this guy walked up to us and told us we sounded great, then asked us to follow him upstairs. When we got there he went into an office while we waited outside. Marvin poked me; he was so excited. 'The cat digs us,' he said. 'Something good's gonna come out of this.' I told Marvin I thought he was right. A few minutes later the man came out of the office and handed us our checks. We'd been fired."

With music still on their minds, Reese began putting together another group. He had already rounded up Chester Simmons, who had earlier sung with the Rainbows, and James Nolan. Now, with Marvin available, the tenor spot was filled. The new group would be called the Marquees.

It didn't take long for the Marquees to make an impression locally through appearances in clubs and on television. Knowing that Marvin wanted to sing really didn't anger Father, but he was upset over the kind of music Marvin wanted to sing—and was singing. "We don't shake that way for the Lord," he kept mumbling. At home, we always knew when and where Marvin would be singing with the Marquees. Father wouldn't let us have a television set at home, so if we wanted to see Marvin on the Milt Grant Show, for example, we'd go visit a friend or neighbor.

It was at Peasie's apartment that Marvin met Elias McDaniel, who had made a name for himself as Bo Diddley. Peasie's sister was a huge fan of Bo; she had come to know him by hanging out backstage whenever he performed at the Howard Theater in D.C. As it turned out, however, Peasie's sister wasn't the only connection to Bo Diddley. Chester Simmons was also working for Bo as his valet and driver.

Bo had created a buzz in the music business two years earlier, in 1955, with the release of "Bo Diddley," his first single. Born in Chicago, with its postwar blues sounds, he knew the music business, especially since the coming of rock 'n' roll. Now he was living in D.C., in a house with his own recording studio, on Rhode Island Avenue.

When Bo first met the Marquees he wasn't really familiar with the group. But after he heard the guys sing at Peasie's apartment, they began showing up at his house whenever possible to jam, rap, or listen to Bo talk. Marvin, who was ten years younger than Bo, even visited Bo's place on his own to record practice tapes using new material of Bo's.

Bo Diddley had so much confidence in the Marquees that he got the group an audition with OKeh Records, a subsidiary of Columbia Records. Reese Palmer remembers, "OKeh wanted to put us under contract, but there was a problem. Marvin was underage, not yet twenty-one, and he couldn't sign for himself. That meant his father had to sign for him, and his father wouldn't do it. He wouldn't let Mrs. Gay sign either, so I forged his father's signature.

"I said to Marvin, 'How do you spell your daddy's name?' and he told me, 'Same as mine, man. I'm a junior. What's you up to?' I looked at Marvin, smiled, and said, 'Don't worry about it, Bro. I got it.' "

It wasn't many days later that Father cornered Reese on the street. Reese says, "He was always getting on me about something because he thought I was leading Marvin astray. It was the other way around."

"I'm not crazy," Father told Reese. "If I'd signed that contract, I'd remember. You signed my name on it, didn't you?"

Reese says he did what most kids do when they get caught. He played dumb. "Who, me?" he answered Father with big, wide eyes. "Mr. Gay didn't know what to do with me so he gave me one of his long, hard looks. Then he shook his head and walked away." Reese now admits that he also signed his own mother's name to his OKeh contract when she refused. "If I'd signed my father's name," he says, "I wouldn't be around today."

On September 25th, 1957, Bo Diddley drove the Marquees— Marvin, Reese Palmer, Chester Simmons, and James Nolan—to

New York to cut "Wyatt Earp" for OKeh Records. The song, a novelty number written by Reese, was one everyone hoped would ride on the popularity of the then extremely successful TV western, "The Life and Legend of Wyatt Earp," starring Hugh O'Brian. Bo not only produced the session, he had his own band back the Marquees.

Marvin prayed his first recording would be a hit, to make Father proud and to earn some money for the family. A hit record would prove to Father that Marvin had ability and that he could be successful on his own—or so Marvin believed. But "Wyatt Earp" went nowhere. Neither did its flip side, "Hey Little School Girl."

The failure had Marvin, Reese, Chester, and James scrounging for work, anything to make some money. Marvin had really never held a job before. The brief stint at the Hot Shop Commissary didn't count. And when he told people he had caddied part-time at a D.C. country club, no one was impressed. He ended up washing dishes behind the lunch counter at People's Drugstore. It was a while until I heard him say "I hear music" again; he admitted that was impossible with all the rattling of dishes.

Marvin wanted to sing, just sing, nothing else. He was good, and he knew it. He really admired only a handful of singers, most of all Frank Sinatra, his style and his attitude. Sinatra was smooth. Cool. So were Nat Cole; Perry Como; Sammy Davis, Jr.; and Jesse Belvin. Marvin wanted to be like them.

Marvin was going through a period of frustration and indecision. Part of that had to do with having to move back home again when he became a dishwasher, but more because of the Marquees. The group was still together, but barely. The guys hadn't given up, not yet, but Marvin wondered how long they would have to wait for a second chance at stardom. "I'm going to be a star," he'd say, again and again. He said it so often he believed it.

It was during this period of creeping doubt and self-bolstering that Marvin discovered D.C.'s red-light district, a six-block section of town along 14th Street. It wasn't the shady atmosphere that attracted him, although after his experience in the Air Force I began to suspect he was on the hunt again. I was wrong; it wasn't sex that had lured him there, it was the music coming out of the clubs. Early one Thursday evening he asked me to go with him to Diamond Jim's for amateur night. Anyone who wanted to get up and sing could have 15 minutes. I guess I was there for moral support because, for the first time, according to Marvin's memory, he felt he was ready to sing alone in the spotlight, not as a member of a group. Of all the people at Diamond Jim's that night, Marvin was the logical person to step onstage and sing. But he got cold feet. When the time came he couldn't do it. I encouraged him, I begged him, I pushed him; nothing could get him to move out of his chair.

The sad part was that Marvin knew he could do it. He'd done it before, in church numerous times, and in a talent show at William Randall Junior High. Before an assembly of kids his own age he stood at center stage and let loose with his own rendition of "Cry," a song made popular by Johnny Ray, a young white singing sensation. When Ray sang the song, tears ran down his face. When Marvin sang the song no one cried, but the kids whooped and hollered. Audiences were more sympathetic to Johnny Ray, however. He was deaf.

Between William Randall High and Diamond Jim's, something had made Marvin gun-shy as a solo singer. Crowds didn't bother me, so when Marvin wouldn't budge I stepped up to the stage and sang "You Send Me," in my best Sam Cooke voice, and it went over pretty good. When no one threw anything, I told myself, "I guess I won't have to dig ditches."

I thought Marvin would be proud of me, and maybe he was, but all he would say was, "Aw, you did all right." I told him that he was the first in the family to cut a record, but I was first to sing onstage in a nightspot. That bothered him until Harvey Fuqua came along.

Like Bo Diddley, Harvey was older than Marvin. In Harvey's case, 11 years older, which to someone only nineteen was almost ancient. At home, we were taught to respect our elders, but Marvin more than respected Harvey; he idolized him. To Marvin, Harvey was worldly and wise, not only to the ways of the world and life, but about show business, too. A tall, trim man with slicked-back, pomaded hair, Harvey was a singer, songwriter, recording artist, vocal arranger, and keyboard player. He had toured nationally with such headliners as Sarah Vaughan and Muddy Waters, and had appeared in two movies with Alan Freed, the legendary Cleveland disc jockey who has been credited with almost single-handedly creating rock 'n' roll by promoting young black musical talent. It didn't hurt that he was also a Kentuckian, like Father.

Marvin first met Harvey Fuqua between shows at the Howard Theater. He and his group, the Moonglows, had just come offstage when Marvin rushed up to congratulate them. "I love you guys," he gushed, then started to babble on. Harvey excused himself to get a bite to eat during the break, but Marvin didn't leave. He accepted an invitation from one of the Moonglows to the group's dressing room, and there he was when Harvey returned.

Marvin wasn't shy when it came to pushing the Marquees. "I'm in a group too," he told Harvey. "Can you help us?" A year earlier, Harvey probably wouldn't have paid any attention to Marvin. Now he was interested in what Marvin had to say. He wanted to hear the Marquees sing.

The Moonglows were the most successful doo wop group in America for a time. They'd had hit after hit, including Marvin's favorite, "The Ten Commandments of Love," on which Harvey sang lead. But the Moonglows' popularity had slipped recently, and there was dissension within the group. One of the members had drug problems. Others complained about not having songwriter credits on their hit singles, and about lack of payments. Rehearsals had become a disaster. It would be only a matter of weeks, perhaps days, before the group split up.

Harvey heard the Marquees sing and was impressed. The Marquees became the new Moonglows around the end of 1958.

Much has been written about Father's reaction to Marvin hooking up with Harvey, and the possibility of Marvin leaving home with Harvey and the Moonglows. The truth is, once Marvin became a Moonglow, there were only a couple of tense moments, and they had nothing to do with Harvey or the music. This time it was show business.

Father and Marvin had a number of "chats" on the subject. Only it was Father who did all the chatting, and once he hit on a subject he hammered it home. "How many parents want their child to get into show business?" he asked, a slight smile crossing his face. 'You want to *what?*' they ask. 'Oh, Lord, what did we do wrong? I planned for my little boy to be a doctor and he wants to sing. Please forgive me.'" Father laughed at his little dramatic reenactment, but he didn't stop. "No parent wants a child to go into show business," he said. "It's a hard road and few people make it 'cause it's the roughest business in the world. It's like walking across quicksand. You might make it if you go fast enough, but there are very few people who don't sink along the way. One way or another, it'll get you."

There was more, and it was a sore subject with Father. It started during Marvin's time with the Marquees and continued when he was with the Moonglows, and that was because of Marvin's failure at times to obey house rules when rehearsing. Marvin was usually good about getting home by ten o'clock, his specified curfew hour, but there were times when he could not. Marvin was still underage, not yet twenty-one, and Father continued to hold a tight rein on all us kids. We knew that as long as we lived under his roof we had to follow his rules.

One evening, Father got especially upset. Before Marvin had left he had reminded him to get home before the curfew or he would find the doors locked. Ten o'clock came and went, and no Marvin. Father locked the doors, then stayed up to wait for him. Marvin returned around midnight but he couldn't get in. He stayed outside for a while, then he wandered off. Mother was frantic. She sent me to look for him but he wasn't anywhere around.

Marvin didn't return until the next morning, and he wasn't alone. He came with Harvey; he had stayed with him all night. Father was surprisingly receptive. He knew he couldn't whip Marvin anymore, he was too big for that, and his last attempt to control him had failed. So Father, Marvin, and Harvey sat down and talked. At one point, Marvin told Father, "I may never be a doctor or a lawyer, a mechanic, a poet, or even a Panther, but I'll succeed. You have to do your thing if you want to be a winner."

"The Bible tells us what's going to happen," Father replied. "There are no surprises. If you know your Bible, and I pray you do, the road you're choosing is not only wrong but impossible."

"But if you're doing what everyone else is doing," said Marvin, "you're going to be led down the same path. I'm not like everyone."

With a thin smile, Father replied, "When my parents got through teaching me, I was the best I would ever be in life. No drinking, no smoking, no cursing, and I ate right. You have the rest of your life to tear yourself down. Now you can destroy yourself, if that is your choice."

Marvin thought for a moment, then said, "I can never forget all you've taught me. You've always been my greatest influence, and that's what's pushing me to be myself. I need to do this with Harvey. I need to try."

Father looked at Harvey, then back at Marvin. He liked Harvey Fuqua, at least enough to turn Marvin over to him. Father said to Harvey, "If Marvin wants to go—and I feel better having him go with you—don't just let him run wild. Train him, teach him."

Father did not kick Marvin out of the house. And Marvin did not run off with Harvey against Father's wishes. Marvin left home with Father's approval. He also carried with him Father's prayer for a good life. Father did not embrace Marvin as he readied to leave; he had already shown his love for Marvin by saying what he did to Harvey. Now I wondered how Mother would react. She loved to hear him sing and express himself with his music, but a career in music? She feared what her churchgoing friends would think. In time, however, she saw how much music truly meant to Marvin and she came around to his side. Father couldn't. He was held by the laws of the Bible. "Right is right," he would mumble, "and wrong is wrong." But as Marvin was about to slip away with Harvey, Mother reached out to him and they wrapped their arms around each other. Then she said, "Go on, my boy, make something of yourself."

5

*H*arvey and Marvin, along with the other members of the Moonglows, headed for Chicago, where they moved into an apartment on 57th and Woodlawn. It wasn't long before Harvey added another member to the group, making it a sextet. With addition of Chuck Barksdale, who had been singing with the Dells, the new Moonglows were named Harvey and the Moonglows.

Their landlords were Phil and Leonard Chess, who owned Harvey's record label, Chess. Early on, most of the group's time was spent backing other artists who passed through Chicago. It wasn't long after Marvin left home that I received a letter from him telling me to listen for a new Chuck Berry record called "Back in the USA." "That's me singing harmony!" he proudly wrote.

Marvin, with Harvey and the Moonglows, sang on another Chuck Berry record, "Almost Grown," and when a young rhythm and blues singer named Etta James recorded "Chained to My Rocking Chair," Marvin sang on that as well. Etta had gained attention four years earlier, in 1955, with "Dance with Me Henry," a song she had introduced and cowrote with Johnny Otis and Hank Ballard.

Singing backup on someone else's songs wasn't quite what Marvin wanted to be doing. It was a start, however, and he believed that his chance would come eventually. That chance did come when he was asked to sing lead on the Moonglows' recording of "Mama Loochie," a song Marvin cowrote with Harvey. It was the first record on which Marvin's solo voice was heard, and he sent a copy home to me. I rushed out of the house and over to Buddy Comedy's, where we played the life out of it. I couldn't stop thinking and saying, "That's my brother!" What that song was about, we had no idea. We doubted if Marvin did either, but he made up a good enough story for us. "It's about marriage, raising kids, happiness," he said. Sounded good, the way he said it, but how would Father take it? I couldn't tell him, not when Marvin used words like "coochie" to rhyme with "loochie."

Having his voice on a few recordings made Marvin feel like his career was on the upswing, even though none of the recordings made much of an impression. He was busy doing what he liked to do, but not too busy to find time to catch the eye of a shake dancer named Toni, who worked with the Moonglows while they were on tour. Being on the road was a first for Marvin; getting together with another prostitute, which I heard was Toni's sideline occupation, was not.

"I'm in love," Marvin confessed one day midway between gigs. His voice sounded dreamy and soft, much like he was crooning a love song. Marvin had never been in love before, so this feeling was all new to him. I was hoping he'd find someone he could be close to, someone who could make him really happy. But after learning more about Toni—her professional name was "Titty Tassel Toni"—I began to have my doubts she was the one. Marvin admitted that she had turned him on to marijuana, which, coming from my God-fearing brother, was a shocker. Now there was more about Marvin I had to hide from the family. The list was growing.

The next time I heard from Marvin he didn't sound quite so mellow when I asked about Toni. "She's a little spitfire," he replied, "definitely much more than a handful."

"Trouble?"

"Ha!" he laughed in my ear. "But nothing we can't work out . . . I hope."

Hoping wasn't enough, apparently, because his affair with Toni went downhill fast, which may have been another sign of things to come. Marvin had a hard time in his relationships with ladies, even though he loved them and loved being with them. His voice, his manner, his looks certainly attracted the opposite sex in numbers, but his stubbornness, his ego, and his jealous nature too often created problems that forced them away. He was much more comfortable, he admitted, standing or sitting with the group, in front of a crowd of ladies, loving them from a distance.

The tour, which took Harvey and the Moonglows deep into the South, was an eye-opener for Marvin in other ways, as well. He was looking forward to performing with the group before large crowds in big auditoriums and theaters, places on a par with the Howard Theater in D.C. But all I heard about were "sweaty dancehalls and dingy dives that smell like they've never been aired out."

Except for the taunting we'd received as kids about our names and religion and way of life, Marvin and I had never really felt prejudice. We'd heard about discrimination, and we knew what was going on outside of Washington, D.C., but the nation's capital had to be unrestricted. Too many dignitaries came to D.C. from around the world, all races and nationalities, and they couldn't confront signs saying "Whites Only" or "Blacks Only." What would the president of Nigeria think?

For me, living where we did, going to all-black segregated schools seemed natural. Our whole neighborhood was black. But things were different across the state lines. "Don't cross those lines," neighbors warned us. "Don't go outside the borders, especially to Maryland and Virginia. The laws are way different, so have fun while you're here."

Being on the road with Harvey and the group was indeed a whole different way of life. "Somewhere in the South," Marvin said, "we pulled in to a gas station, and the attendant, one of those good ol' boys, paid no mind to us. He just sat in his rocking chair with a look like, 'I wonder what they want, 'cause they ain't gettin' none of it here.'

"You may get something if you say 'sir,' " Marvin went on, "or you knuckle under and talk Southern, but even that doesn't work if you have a New York or some other kind of Yankee license plate."

Marvin told tales of being refused service at cafes along the highway, as well as in restaurants where they stopped to perform, in such cities as Louisville and Houston. There were times when they wound up eating out of cans before going onstage, then sleeping in their station wagon or under the stars because they weren't allowed in most hotels, even cheap motels.

Reese Palmer remembers touring with Marvin and the Moonglows. Says Reese, "We were in Jacksonville, Florida, in the backyard of a house where we were all staying, and Harvey was putting chemicals in Marvin's and my hair. Those were the days when black people did that to make their hair straight, to give it that slicked-back, shiny, patent-leather look. So Harvey was doing Marvin and me at the same time, and he told us to leave the chemicals in until we felt a burning in our scalp. That's when, he told us, we should wash out the chemicals in either cold or warm water.

"When we felt our scalps starting to burn, we ran in the house and leaned over the tub, but nothing came out the spigot. Harvey had turned off the water! We were yelling and screaming, we didn't know what to do, and it was burning so bad. We knew of only one place where there was water, and that was a pond not too far from where we were. So we ran outside, still screaming, and jumped into the pond with our clothes on. Our scalps stopped burning but I'm sure all the fish died."

Another time, in Atlanta, Reese remembers, "I was always on Marvin to be careful who he was fucking. For some reason, he was happiest around hookers or somebody's wife who was cutting out. 'Someday you're going to catch something if you keep on doing these women you shouldn't be doing,' I'd tell him. He'd say, 'I'm a soldier, baby. *I* can handle it.' One day we were in a hotel lobby and we went into the bathroom. We were standing a couple of stalls away from each other when I heard him scream, a long, loud scream. 'Man, what the hell is wrong with you?' I asked. He gulped and replied, 'One of those rotten bitches gave me the clap!' That's when I let him have it. 'You? Oh, Lord, you told me you were a soldier. Now you're going to have to go and have the needle.' Marvin's mouth opened, and kept dropping. 'Let me tell you something,' I went on. 'It's going to be a bitch when you go to the clinic. They take your dick and they put it on a table that rises up to the level of your dick. And, man, this is the part that's fucked up. They take a hammer, a big, goddamn hammer and hit you on the head of your dick, and that shit shoots out all over you.' Marvin screamed again. 'Stop acting like a pussy, man, 'cause that's what you got to do.' Marvin was trembling with fright. A few days later he was trembling with anger; he had found out that I was playing with him. He looked at me hard, but all he could say was, 'Stay away from me, man, just stay away.' "

That wasn't the end of their friendship, far from it. Says Reese, "Marvin and I got into more trouble than anybody else in the group. We were always into some shit. Like another time in Atlanta. I won't go into the details, but we had just got through playing at the Pea-cock Club and I had talked with my wife. She wanted me to send some money home and we really weren't making any. When I told Marvin, he came up with an idea. 'What kind of idea?' I wanted to know. He wouldn't tell me then, but he motioned for me to follow him. We went up to our room at the motel where we were staying, shut the door, and he turned the radio up loud so nobody could hear us. 'You know how the TV works?' he asked. 'Yeah,' I said, 'you gotta put a quarter in it.' He went on to explain that there were a whole bunch of quarters in the rooms that were vacant. All we had to do was get them. I told him he was crazy to even think about something like that in the South. 'You want to get us locked up?' I asked him. 'You must be a damn fool!' It was either that, he told me, or have my wife calling every day about money for the baby. I guess I was the damn fool, 'cause we did it, and the motel manager caught us. He told Harvey to get us out of town or we were going to jail. What a choice. We got the hell out of Atlanta."

Marvin was so good about calling his family from the road to let us know how he was doing. We all wanted to know, even Father, but he wouldn't admit it. Of course, Marvin never filled us in on any of the fun stuff. He stuck pretty much to where they were playing and how the shows went over. Then almost a week went by with no call, and I was starting to worry. When he finally did get to us he hemmed and hawed to start, then he blurted out, "We got busted." That was quickly followed with, "But everything is okay now, we're all fine."

"What do you mean—" I almost repeated "busted," but I didn't want anyone else in the house to hear that word. "What happened?" I asked instead.

"It was probably a racial thing because we weren't doing nothin'."

"What?" I asked. "What are you talking about?"

"We were on our way to a club date in Corpus Christi when we parked in a town called Beaumont. We all got out for a break and somebody called the cops on us."

"Why?"

"You have to understand how it is around these parts. We were just stretching our legs, I swear, then we piled back in the cars and took off."

"I thought you said somebody called the cops."

"They did, but we didn't see them until we were on the road again. They tailed us down the highway, cop cars with their lights going and sirens wailing, so we pulled over. Then they made us get out and they searched us."

"Yeah?"

"Well, they found some stuff."

"What kind of stuff?"

"Just stuff."

"On you?"

"Naw, in one of the cars."

"What kind of stuff?" I repeated.

"You know, a little grass, a couple of joints. They said they found some other stuff, but I think they planted that. I can believe the grass but not the heavier stuff."

"That's no good, Marvin. What did they do to you? Where are you?"

"They took us back to Beaumont, held us a few hours, and..."

"You were arrested? You were in jail?"

"Well, they charged us with vagrancy, made us pay a fine, and let us go. The bad thing is..."

"There's more? It's worse?"

"Some reporters showed up at the courthouse. Harvey's worried there may be some bad publicity about us. But you never know. The way things are going, some bad publicity might be better than nothing at all." Marvin chuckled at his last remark. He obviously wasn't taking the encounter with the Texas police too seriously, or he was playing it down for me.

As the tour neared its end, and the group headed back up north, I heard from Marvin again. At the sound of his voice I mumbled to myself, "Good news, please."

Marvin and the others were frustrated and angry, and when Marvin was upset, he babbled. "We've passed through states where you don't even want to stop. You keep looking at the gas gauge to make sure you have enough in the tank ... or you're checking the speedometer to make sure you're going under the speed limit. What am I saying? Forget speeding. They'll get you one way or the other ... two hundred dollars per person, for just being there."

"Not again," I said.

Marvin sighed. "Oh, man. It's like these guys are just sitting by the side of the road, checking cars, looking for out-of-state license plates. Then they see one and say, 'Let's get him.' It doesn't matter who you are as long as you're a stranger. Then those good ol' boys change hats—from mechanic or pump jockey to sheriff to judge. That's how they make their money. You hear these things and you hope they're not true."

"You didn't get stopped again?"

"We're clean, man, but that don't really mean anything. We're still looking over our shoulders every mile of the way."

"When will you be back?"

"We're on our way," he answered hurriedly. "Gotta go. Give Mother a hug." The next sound was a click, and the phone went dead.

A week or so later I heard over the radio that Harvey and the Moonglows were coming to Washington, D.C. They were opening for Mary Ann Fisher, a fine singer who had worked with Ray Charles at the Howard Theater. "Marvin's coming home!" I cried out as Mother returned from work. "He's coming here."

"What's wrong?" she asked, looking all worried. "What happened?"

"Nothing's wrong," I said, half-smiling. "Everything's good. They're all coming to sing in town." Had Mother heard something about the group's tour, I wondered. If she had, she said nothing.

"Thank the Lord," Mother replied.

"Maybe he'll be staying here while he's around."

Mother loved that idea but Marvin didn't come home. He couldn't, he said, because of his busy schedule. He and the group were set to do two shows a night, the last one ending around two in the morning. In between, he had rehearsals. But we did get an invitation to one of his shows, which excited me more than anything. It would be my first chance to see Marvin perform professionally.

The invitation was for the whole family, which was Marvin's way of showing Father that he was making it by doing what he wanted to do. Father didn't really want to know, and he certainly didn't want to see or hear what was taking place on the stage at the Howard Theater. He wouldn't stop the rest of us from going, but he refused to come along. As much as he wanted Marvin to be happy and successful, he could not show his approval by attending. "Too much booty-shaking," was his comment.

Had Father gone, he would have had to eat his words. We all loved the show. In fact, seeing Marvin onstage gave me goose bumps. But we couldn't rave to Father; he wouldn't have listened to us even if we did.

From D.C., Harvey and the Moonglows drove to the last stop on the tour: Detroit, Michigan. Long known as America's Motor City, for its automobile production (General Motors, Ford, and Chrysler), Detroit was fast taking on the new nickname of Music City, thanks to its homegrown roster of established and upcoming singers and musicians, performers such as Margaret Whiting, Della Reese, Little Willie John (one of Marvin's idols), Sam Cooke, Freda Payne, Smokey Robinson, and the Miracles. For the final week of shows at Detroit's Twenty Grand Club, Harvey put out a call to friends in the area, inviting them to hear his new Moonglows. One of the people he asked was Berry Gordy, Jr., who arrived with his sisters, Anna and Gwen.

Thirty-year-old Berry Gordy was an energetic and industrious jack-of-all-trades, having dabbled in boxing, merchandising (with his 3-D Record Mart), assembly line work (at Ford), and songwriting—he was best known for his work with Jackie Wilson. He was now beginning to make a name for himself in the music business.

Berry Gordy was one of many new faces Marvin met at the Twenty Grand Club. There was no reason for Marvin to remember Berry, or for Marvin to stand out in Berry's mind, either. Why would he? After all, Marvin sang with a group; he was just one of the singers onstage. But that would soon change. They'd meet again within the coming few months.

The Moonglows were getting work, but not really enough. News of the Texas incident had spread within the music business, causing booking agents to think twice before using the group, if they did at all. There were also money problems and individual conflicts within the group. Nor did it help that the public's preference in music was changing. The sounds of the fifties were giving way to the tastes of a new generation of teenagers, and Detroit was leading the way. Harvey must have felt the pressures that faced the Moonglows, because a short time later he broke up the group, keeping only Marvin with him. He had plans for Marvin, and they didn't include forming another group with Marvin in the spotlight. He wanted Marvin to be *always* in the spotlight. It was time, he said, and Marvin was all for it.

Marvin had made a pact with Harvey, in front of Father, when he left home. He trusted Harvey. If Harvey said he was ready, he was ready. He would follow Harvey anywhere. When Harvey said they were moving to Detroit, Marvin packed the few things he kept in their Chicago apartment, and they were on their way.

Harvey had my brother dreaming again. His plans for Marvin were exactly what Marvin had in mind all along. "Remember what we used to talk about?" he asked, excitedly. "Harvey's saying the same things now, that I have what it takes to be the black Frank Sinatra. If I sing Sinatra's kind of songs, the way I've always wanted to sing them, I know I can make it. And Harvey's behind me all the way. I can get up anywhere and do that, I know I can."

"I know you can, too," I told him. "You can sing the stuffing out of those songs. The ladies will go crazy. Everyone will."

"Even Father. No way he can roar up over those songs. They're sweet, and loving, and sexy in a good way. No booty-shaking, no hoochie-coochie. It's all good."

Reaching Detroit, Harvey and Marvin found a small apartment, then Harvey looked for work in the music business. He landed a job as a talent scout with Leonard Chess, at Chess Records, but he soon became unhappy with his set hours, all in the office, starting at 10 A.M. Being an entertainer, he was accustomed to late hours, sleep-in mornings, and more freedom. "Leonard was real understanding," said Harvey. "He told me to check with Billy Davis and Gwen Gordy, at Anna Records. 'If you want to be free, go there,' Leonard told me. 'You can come in when you want, go on the road, produce records. You'll be helping to build a new label.'"

Harvey already had one foot in the door at Anna Records. He knew Billy Davis, a songwriter who had cowritten the song "See-Saw" for the original Moonglows. Gwen Gordy, his business partner and lover, was the sister of Berry Gordy. Billy and Berry had also worked together writing songs.

Billy offered Harvey a job with Anna Records. Harvey accepted, bringing Marvin with him. Within a few months, Harvey started his own label, which was immodestly named Harvey Records. "The label was especially created for Marvin," Harvey said. That was easy to believe. Aside from Marvin, Harvey had signed only one other solo artist, a sax player named Junior Walker, as well as a group called the Quails.

Once inside Anna Records, Harvey began to work fast. He had eyes for Gwen Gordy, and it wasn't long before her affections for Billy began sliding Harvey's way. "Harvey was looking to improve himself," said Marvin, who was suddenly seeing Harvey in a new light.

Almost as suddenly, Harvey Records hooked up with Anna Records. Marvin began to wonder where his career was headed, now that Harvey had a new interest. He hadn't recorded for Harvey Records, and Harvey had stopped talking about "the black Sinatra." Anna Records (named for Gwen's sister, Anna Gordy) already had a list of talented artists, such as Barrett Strong, the Spinners, and Joe Tex. Marvin worried about that.

It was hard enough to keep track of what was going on at the office of Anna Records, but there was just as much action, or more, going on down the road. With eight hundred dollars borrowed from his family's savings, and more than a little encouragement from his closest friend, singer-songwriter William "Smokey" Robinson, Berry Gordy had turned the basement of his windowless two-story house into a recording studio. It had soundproof walls (which really weren't, according to Marvin), a control room, a cubicle large enough for one singer, used recording equipment, and microphones hanging from overhead cables. Berry Gordy the song publisher was now a music publisher and owner of a small recording company. (His sister Gwen had done it, so why couldn't he?) Smokey Robinson became the first artist he signed.

Berry's Motown Record Corporation actually got its start in 1959, with the creation of the Tamla label, an offshoot of Motown. Berry had wanted to name it Tammy, after Debbie Reynolds's big hit record from her 1957 movie, *Tammy and the Bachelor,* but someone had already used the name. A white singer-actress had inspired his label, but he was clearly in business to celebrate Detroit's rhythmic new sounds of black music, as well as its singers, songwriters, and musicians. And, not so surprisingly, to make a profit for himself.

By the end of 1960, Motown held its first Christmas party, attended by its growing staff and their family and friends. Marvin was there too, off in a dim corner working the piano as if he were the entertainment in a smoky lounge. At one point, Gwen Gordy told him she wanted him to meet her brother, Berry. Marvin politely said, "Some other time," and kept playing. She came back to his side several more times, but he wouldn't leave the piano. A short time later he looked up to find Berry Gordy standing next to him.

Our phone rang at home early the next morning. It was Marvin calling from Detroit to fill me in about the party, and to tell me he'd talked with Berry Gordy. "Neither of us made any mention that we'd met before when I was one of the Moonglows," he said. "I tried to be cool, so I kept playing, real softly. Then he asked me if I'd do something for him, and without missing a beat, I gave him a real dreamy version of "Mr. Sandman," you know, that song made popular by the Chordettes, only I slowed it way down and put more soul into it."

"What did he say?" I asked.

"He liked it. He even said I have something special. He wants to talk."

"When?"

"I don't know, but I have a feeling something big is about to happen."

Marvin also had a feeling Harvey had something up his sleeve. He was right. Needing money, Harvey made a deal with Berry, who was expressing real interest in my brother. Without consulting Marvin, Harvey sold Berry all the talent he had signed to his Harvey Records label, including Marvin.

When Marvin teamed up with Harvey, it was understood they would be tied together for all time. Now Harvey had sold him out, but the rope wasn't completely cut. Harvey didn't sell all of Marvin, only 50 percent, which meant he could still manage Marvin and make a profit off of him. Marvin never forgot his friend and mentor's betrayal. The memory of Harvey's deal, possibly pushed through to impress his girlfriend, Gwen Gordy, stayed with Marvin always.

As it turned out, Harvey and Gwen got married, while Berry got a future star at Motown.

6

Berry Gordy wasn't the only person at Motown who thought Marvin had star potential. Although Gwen Gordy had pushed her brother into hearing Marvin sing, it was Anna Gordy who really brought him into the Motown family.

Anna had first seen Marvin at the offices of Anna Records, the label that sister Gwen had named after her, and she liked what she saw. Marvin liked what he saw too, and he began to stop by her desk every afternoon at the same time. What began as flirtatious and playful soon turned serious, another landmark in the romance department for Marvin: his first true love. Within only two months after they had met, Marvin and Anna were living together in her apartment.

Marvin and Anna were a good match, probably because they were complete opposites. She was so many things he wasn't. Anna was outgoing; Marvin was shy. She was confident; he was inwardly unsure of himself. She was experienced; he was not. She was also a beautiful lady, fun, supportive, ambitious, and well-connected; she knew who was who in and around Detroit. It didn't matter that Anna was 17 years older than Marvin, which led to more teasing for him. "Let people say I'm dating my mother," he said. "I don't care what they say. I love her, and she calls me her new star."

Despite Marvin's solid connection with the Gordys, little was happening to further his singing career. Years later he remarked about his early days at Motown, "I was simply paying my dues, hanging out until closing time, then helping carry out the trash, clean up the dishes, and get ready for the next day. I would have paid them to hire me out or let me play piano or drums in the studio, help write songs, or whatever, because I was extremely anxious about getting into show business."

It wasn't all sitting around. Marvin filled in as the drummer on a few sessions, and he sang backup on many of the early Tamla releases. There was more, something else that all the Motown artists were put through, and Marvin credited Anna with getting it going: the company's charm school. Anna always dressed beautifully, walked with style, and turned heads when she walked into a room. She felt the artists on the roster needed help in many areas. Most of the talented young performers had come from the inner city and were somewhat rough around the edges, a little underdone. Their diction, grooming, fashion and style, manners, poise, body language, stage presence, and possibly more, required attention. No more street talk, no slouching, no strutting, no gum-chewing. In a word, Anna and her brother felt that everyone who represented Motown had to be "classy" whenever they appeared before the public.

Mrs. Maxine Powell was hired to run Motown's new charm school. Marvin hated the idea at first. Here was someone else telling him what to do, and the thought of attending classes again made his head pound. "Oh, Lord," he moaned. "They have me going back to school again. All I want to do is sing!" Once he started, however, he kind of glided through. He had a head start in manners, and he certainly knew how to put on the charm, from the way we were brought up at home. The only class that gave him fits was dancing, where he was a total clod. Marvin couldn't move his feet. He had a hard time walking, let alone dancing; his feet had always been bad. Making him look graceful was a real challenge for his teacher. Smokey Robinson had taken to calling Marvin "Dad" early on, because his walk reminded Smokey of an old man.

Between classes, cleaning, and backup work on recordings, Marvin was kept busy, but not too busy to vent his frustrations to Berry Gordy. Marvin was growing increasingly restless, over-the-top edgy, more and more impossible to deal with, and that came across in our conversations. Since moving to Detroit, not a day passed that he didn't call home. I could hear the tension growing in his voice with each call.

Berry had apparently heard enough from Marvin, at least to get his young singer in the studio. At this point he still didn't really know how to present Marvin. But Marvin knew, as always, that he wanted to have things his own way. He wasn't right for rock 'n' roll or rhythm and blues, or even the emerging Motown sound, with its pounding backbeat. His best bet to reach a broad commercial audience, he felt, wasn't dance music but romantic standards written by the great American songwriters like Irving Berlin, Richard Rodgers and Lorenz Hart, Ira and George Gershwin, Harold Arlen, Cole Porter, and Jerome Kern. He wanted to follow in the footsteps of his singing idols.

Some, months earlier, Berry had him record a promotional demonstration single. On one side of the disc was "The Masquerade Is Over," by Herb Magidson and Allie Wrubel, the team that had written, among other songs, the huge Harry James–Kitty Kallen hit, "I'll Buy That Dream." The flip side of the single was "Witchcraft," written by Carolyn Leigh and Cy Coleman, for Frank Sinatra. The label credited Marvin Gay as the vocalist.

Now, back in the recording studio again to record his first commercially released single, Berry Gordy let Marvin have his way, for the most part. During the session, Marvin recorded no fewer than nine songs, seven by some of his favorite songwriters. The remaining two songs included one by Berry, as well as one by Anna Gordy and Harvey Fuqua. How could Marvin say no to that?

Unfortunately, Marvin's first single had the two worst songs. The A-side, a low-key attempt at rhythm and blues called "Let Your Conscience Be Your Guide," was written and produced by Berry. Marvin said, "I was eager to do anything just to be recording, but I got a real lemon to get things going—here's someone who'd written 'Shop Around,' 'I'll Be Satisfied,' 'Lonely Teardrops,' and 'Reet Petite,' and yet I wound up with 'Let Your Conscience Be Your Guide.' In all fairness, though, maybe it was me. Maybe I didn't do a good job." The B-side, "Never Let You Go (Sha-Lu-Bop)," written by Anna and Harvey, was just as forgettable.

The only good thing that came from the release of that record was a sort of name change for Marvin—and even then he wasn't happy. The label credited Marvin Gaye. Same name, same pronunciation, new spelling. "They put an 'e' on the end of 'Gay,'" he complained. "Can you believe that? What does that do for me? Just put an 'is' in front and what do you have? Same old thing!" Still, he had to admit it was different. I liked it. When Marvin added an "e," so did I.

In June 1961, a month after the release of Marvin's first single, Tamla gathered all 11 of his songs from the recording session and issued his first album, *The Soulful Moods of Marvin Gaye.* He was thrilled about that, believing that now the public would get to hear him singing some of the great standards, songs he'd wanted to sing all along. Included were a Rodgers and Hart standard ("My Funny Valentine"), two songs by Irving Berlin ("How Deep Is the Ocean" and "Always"), and one each by Cole Porter ("Love for Sale"), Leo Robin and Ralph Rainger ("Easy Living"), and Don Raye and Gene De-Paul ("You Don't Know What Love Is"). There were also the songs from his earlier promotional disc and his first single.

The album was a flop. The label wanted to promote Marvin as the new Sam Cooke, even the new Nat "King" Cole, but he had the new Frank Sinatra in mind and wouldn't cooperate. The folks at Motown were trying to help. All Marvin was doing, except complaining, was hurting himself.

The phone rang at home. At first all I could hear was background noise, a distant blur of people talking, laughing, and moving around. "Frankie," he said, "it's me."

"What?" I replied.

"It's me," he repeated. His voice was so soft I could barely hear him.

"What's going on?" I asked. "Where are you?"

"At Cunningham's Drug Store, down the street from Motown ... or 'Hitsville,' they're calling it now."

"Hitswhat?"

"Hitsville," he repeated. "They've put a big sign up over the front of the place."

"Why are you calling from a drugstore? And talk louder."

"I don't want nobody to hear me."

"What's wrong?"

"I'm hurtin', man, that's what."

"What's happening?"

"Nothin', that's what."

"You've got it all going for you. You're working, you're on a label, you're recording, you're doing good."

Marvin sighed. "It sounds better than it is ... and it's not good. My records aren't taking off. I need a hit in a bad way."

"It'll happen. You just gotta be patient. It'll come."

"Maybe I'm not good enough at doin' what I want to do. Maybe Berry's right."

"About what?"

"He never did want me crooning. Now he's got proof. He said it ain't working. That sounds like now I'm supposed to follow what he says and do what he wants me to do. Kind of like being at home."

"Don't mess things up, Marvin."

"Man, I don't know which way to turn. Maybe it was me, the way I did it, but I have a feeling if they'd pushed my songs the way

I wanted, things would be different. Get me into the record stores and with the DJs, and *I'll* push. There's no pushing going on."

Marvin was getting a reputation around Hitsville. There were lots of "do this" and "do that" things around the office, he said, like the charm school classes. There were also all the meetings with salespeople, writers, and producers. "This is the meetingest place on earth," he complained. "Meetings, meetings, meetings! They meet to talk, they meet to vote, they meet for everything ... the singers, the songs, the songwriters, the coffee, the weather, paperclips."

Marvin didn't always show up on time for meetings, which had him in the doghouse more than once. Berry had a rule. Anyone five minutes late to a meeting would be locked out. Marvin often found himself outside the meeting room, unable to get in. It wasn't that his watch was always running slow, it was that he had his own way of doing things, which didn't surprise me. I was the follower, not Marvin.

His rebellious attitude actually turned things around for him. Whether he heard talk in the office or from Anna at home, I don't know, but he told me he had started playing around with a song that didn't sound like the old standards, music Smokey called "cornball," but had more of a pop sound. Berry liked what he heard, suggested some chord changes, then brought in Mickey Stevenson, a writer-producer for the company. The collaboration resulted in "Stubborn Kind of Fellow." With Martha Reeves and the Vandellas singing backup for Marvin, the record became a hit, reaching No. 8 on the R&B charts.

Although "Stubborn Kind of Fellow" wasn't the crossover hit Marvin was hoping for—it topped, at No. 46 on the pop charts—he was thrilled with the record's success. Perhaps best of all, in his eyes, was that the song had made a personal statement. "You're gettin' it, aren't you?" he asked me one day. "It's all about me. *It's all about me!* Not many people will probably get it, but I knew you would."

For anyone who knew Marvin, it was impossible not to connect the song with him. His ego had gotten a big boost, and there would be a lot more of that in the future. And while he didn't re-alize it at the time, his direction as a singer-songwriter would defi-nitely change. All he knew now, however, was that the success of "Stubborn Kind of Fellow" had him looking at his choice of ma-terial in a new way. He still felt he was meant to be a crooner, and he was determined to sing and record more "cornball" standards, if only to please Father. But if R&B would get him where he wanted to go, he was going in that direction.

New directions were definitely in Marvin's future. Before the end of the year, he and all the Motown performers would be hit-ting the road for the first Motortown Revue. The thought of hav-ing to get back onstage, this time as a single act before crowds of fans, had him nearly paralyzed with fear. But Marvin had to be a star, and he knew that came with a price; singing live was the price he had to pay.

The Motortown Revue, or Motown Revue, as it came to be known, was the brainchild of Berry Gordy. It was a new concept in the music industry. Never before had a record company gathered to-gether its stable of stars and sent them out to perform in concert. Many of the solo singers and groups had at least one hit record, while others were less well-known, but by the end of the tour, thousands of record buyers would know them all, and offers would be coming in for various acts to appear on television and in nightclubs.

The tour would take in 34 cities over a two-month period, mostly one-nighters with stops along the East Coast, down through the South's "chitlin circuit," then back up north. Because of the shoe-string budget, anything west of the Mississippi River was out. Even on paper, the constant traveling and performing—five to seven shows a day in some places—looked to be grueling. Getting from here to there in an old scrap-yard school bus plastered with signs that read "Motor City Tour" didn't bring smiles to anyone, especially since it lacked all creature comforts, including a bathroom and sleeping facil-ities. Because of the long distances between venues, the 35 travelers were often forced to sleep in their seats or on the overhead baggage

racks. More often than not, they arrived just before showtime looking road-weary and bedraggled.

The first stop on the Motortown Tour was the Howard Theater
in Washington, D.C. It was October 1962, and Mother and I were
there, shaking in our shoes. We were probably more scared than
Marvin, but that was impossible to tell. We purposely got to the theater early to see him, but we couldn't get backstage. Having to wait
made us even more jittery.

By the time the doors opened there was a long line, four and five
people deep, mainly with black, energy-filled young ladies eager to
get inside. There we sat, watching the place fill, while Mother kept
asking, "When's Marvin coming out?" I couldn't tell her. "He'll be
along," was all I could say.

At last the house lights went down, and the crowd started screaming. Mother took my arm and held on tight.

The Supremes came on first. They weren't the Supremes as we
came to know them later. The girls weren't as smooth and polished
as they would be with a little more experience, but they sounded
good, and they looked elegant in their finery.

Then came Martha Reeves and the Vandellas, followed by the
Contours, with their wild, over-the-top energy. The audience
screamed.

"Where's my boy?" Mother asked.

The Marvelettes sang "Mr. Postman," which had become a big
hit for the group. Next was Mary Wells, known as the First Lady of
Motown. Then another of Motown's big-star acts, Smokey Robinson and the Miracles. Other than the Gordys, Smokey was the first
person Marvin had met when he came to Motown. Smokey could
do everything, Marvin said. In fact, he talked so much about Smokey
I felt I knew him. In Marvin's eyes, Smokey was the man!

"Where's my boy?" Mother asked again.

By this time I was wondering that myself. Then there he was,
looking all spiffy and handsome in his dark suit with pegged pants,
a tie, and his hair all slicked back. He could barely look out at the

audience as he stood center stage, not far away from Martha and the Vandellas, his backup singers. The crowd gave him a good reception, a little on the polite side, I thought, but then they really didn't know who Marvin was until he launched into "Stubborn Kind of Fellow." At that point everyone went crazy, jumping up and down, yelling and screaming, reaching for him. Marvin didn't move. He just stood there rather awkwardly, sounding a little shaky as the song came out. No one seemed to care, including Mother, who was near tears, poking as many people as she could and boasting, "That's my boy!"

Marvin wasn't happy with his "zombie" performance. "I was so nervous I thought I was going to keel over ... or puke," he confided later. "I kept wondering how I was going to go through that a zillion more times on the tour."

He did go on again, and he kept getting better and better. He never lost his self-consciousness or fear of live performing, but he learned how to put over a song and look like he was having a good time. Marvin blessed Stevie Wonder for that.

Even as a youngster, "Little Stevie," as he was known at the time, was such a dynamic performer. So talented, so electric. Once he was onstage he let everything go. He was only twelve when the first Motown Revue hit the road, but he could work any crowd into a frenzy.

As soon as the folks at Motown saw that one of their singers was having a problem onstage, they would rework the lineup so that Stevie immediately preceded him or her. The reasoning was simple: no one would dare hold back if they had to follow Stevie's all-out, explosive performance. Marvin's first exposure in the Revue was a disappointment to many, including Marvin, but as the tour progressed he became more confident and polished, and more able to project his God-given sexuality. From then on, the ladies in the audience were screaming the moment they caught sight of him, even before he opened his mouth to sing. His performances were filled with steamy sexual energy. He was totally aware of the effect he was having on the ladies, and not too sheepish to take advantage of it. (The ladies in the

Motown office could vouch for that.) Years later, in 1982, it amused me to read that Marvin had finally come to terms with his sexuality with the release of "Sexual Healing." He knew "what it was for" 20 years before that.

Like Marvin's earlier tour with the Moonglows, traveling was not without incident, especially in the South, where the touring company had dates scheduled from North Carolina, Virginia, and Mississippi to Louisiana, Alabama, and Georgia. Marvin reported that they were forced to use blacks-only restrooms and refused service at lunch counters. Shades were quickly drawn, and "Closed" signs went up when the bus came to some stops. Once, an angry mob of white kids tried to tip over the bus; shots were even fired. Then there was the accident, which led to the death of one of the drivers, a relative of Berry's. Lack of sleep had caused that, however, not foul play.

By the time the tour ended in mid-December, everyone was exhausted but happy to be home for Christmas. Marvin didn't come to his real home, his family home; he spent the holidays with Anna, but it's doubtful he saw much of her. He was busy writing songs and planning his next tour, not with a Motown Revue but with James Brown and the Drifters, the Crystals, Charlie Foxx, and Jimmy Reed. There was also the Motown Christmas party, which was held at Detroit's Graystone Ballroom. Berry had recently purchased the building for two reasons: to open the dance palace to blacks, who had previously been allowed inside only one night a week, and to schedule shows headlining Motown entertainers. One of his early promotions was the Motown Battle of the Stars, which pitted Marvin against "Little Stevie" Wonder.

The competition was basically a challenge in three rounds. First Marvin came out and did his thing, then Stevie performed. Marvin knew he'd be in for a rough evening because Stevie was so talented and versatile. As much as he loved Stevie, Marvin did not want to lose, not to a kid half his age, so he spent hours rehearsing for the Battle. Judging from the applause after the first round, Marvin knew he had to open up a bit, so he moved around onstage, strutting and wiggling, then finally breaking into a dance step of sorts. It wasn't pretty, but the crowd went wild, especially the young ladies.

Marvin was sure he'd be the winner. He even had a surprise up his sleeve for the big third round. Knowing how Stevie could work an audience with his harmonica, which he did, Marvin one-upped him by pulling out a melodica, a giant harmonica that's played not only with the mouth but with fingers on an attached keyboard. He waited for the cheers but heard only boos, which grew louder and more ugly as the seconds passed. At first, Marvin couldn't imagine what he had done wrong, then he realized the audience thought he was making fun of the little blind boy.

Marvin began to sweat, wanting to disappear in a puff of smoke, then hide until everyone was gone. But he gamely stayed onstage, struggling through his song till it was over. He didn't stick around to find out who had won.

It was one of Marvin's worst moments. He felt awful, and he couldn't wait to apologize to Stevie. Stevie got the joke; he actually thought it was funny. "No harm done," he told Marvin. Then he laughed and said, "Besides, I never saw what you did." Joke or not, Berry wasn't amused at hearing the boos aimed at Motown. It was a mistake, he said, pitting Marvin against Little Stevie, or pitting any of his performers against one another, for that matter. As far as Berry was concerned, his Battle of the Stars was history.

Despite the Battle debacle, these were good times, and getting better, for the Motown performers. Marvin had even managed to save some money. Based on his record sales, the reaction from the crowds at the Motown Revues, and his schedule for the new year, he knew his career was on the upswing. "I've finally got something the world wants to hear," he said confidently.

It had long been Marvin's hope to do something special for Mother, and at the same time, make Father proud of him. He had heard of a house for sale on Varnum, in a real nice section of north-

Marvin at 13 in 1952. Even then, he knew he had "it."

The three Gay brothers, Michael, Frankie, and Marvin, in 1961.

Harvey Fuqua (foreground) and the Moonglows in 1959, with (l-r) Chester Simmons, Reese Palmer, James Nolan, Marvin Gaye, and Chuck Barksdale.

Early publicity photo of Marvin.

Crowds line up to see the Motortown Revue at the Fox Theater in Detroit in 1961.

Marvin sent this photo of him and his little poodle, Peppi, home to his mother. It was taken in 1963 during his marriage to Anna.

Thank you Mother & Father, for instilling within the talents God gave you !! I love you very very deeply.

Your Son

A loving note from young Marvin to his mother and father, early in his career.

Marvin's flirtatious singing to the young women in his audiences created problems with Anna during their marriage.

Handbill for the 1964 Motortown Revue shows Marvin in the top spot.

Having fun pool-side as Harvey Fuqua (left) and an unidentified friend toss Marvin into the water.

In 1964, on his first visit to London to promote his records, Marvin happily signs autographs for his new British fans.

Marvin performs at Detroit's swank Twenty Grand's Driftwood Lounge in May 1964. His "Marvin Gaye Revue," produced by Harvey Fuqua, broke all attendance records at the showplace.

Although Marvin had several wonderful singing partners, his duets with Tammi Terrell, starting in 1967, resulted in the greatest number of hits.

Flanked by fringe-bedecked "go-go girls," Marvin sings "I Heard It Through the Grapevine" on national TV in 1968.

THE NATIONAL ACADEMY OF RECORDING ARTS AND SCIENCES

presents this certificate to

MARVIN GAYE

in recognition of

NOMINATION

for the

BEST RHYTHM & BLUES VOCAL PERFORMANCE—MALE

I HEARD IT THROUGH THE GRAPEVINE

for the awards period

1968

MORT L. NASATIR
NATIONAL PRESIDENT

Marvin missed out on a Grammy in 1968, but he was given this certificate for his nomination.

west D.C. The house was big, too big really, since sister Jeanne had gotten married and was no longer living at home with the family.

Getting Mother out of the projects and improving her life was important to Marvin. Now that he'd done that, he couldn't wait to see how we were doing. We had been in the new house only a few days when Marvin was at the door. The place was a mess—boxes of clothes, dishes, linens, this and that, still unpacked, were stacked here and there, making it difficult to walk around, or even sit. All the rooms had been newly painted or wallpapered, and the wood-work was polished to a waxy finish.

Sweetsie and I stood by as Mother rushed to Marvin, held him tightly, and said, "This is so wonderful. I never dreamed I'd find my-self in a place like this. But don't ask me where anything is because I don't know."

Marvin laughed. "It'll all come together," he said. "You'll have it looking like a palace in no time."

"If we never did another thing around here, I'd still feel like I was living in one," she said. "Oh, Marvin, you're such a blessing."

I grabbed Marvin's arm and started to show him around.

"Where's Father?" he asked.

"In his room," Mother said. "He should be out shortly."

"I'll get him," I said. "I'll tell him you're here." As I started down the hallway to Father's room, I could hear Mother, Marvin, and Sweetsie all talking at once.

The door to Father's room was closed, which wasn't a good sign. He was either asleep, drinking, or in a mood, I figured. I knocked anyway. "Marvin's here," I said. He didn't respond so I knocked again. Then I returned to the front of the house to be with the others.

About ten minutes later Father appeared down the hallway. He was wearing a long, silky robe and his bedroom slippers. "Hello, Marvin," he said. "Are you back to stay again?"

"No," Marvin said, "just here to check things out. Had to see how everything's going in the new house. How do you like it?"

"I know you're doing good, Marvin. But I'm wondering, are you trying to let money talk for you?"

"I don't understand, Father," Marvin said.

Father nodded. "Let me put it this way, Son. A flower gives off its aroma to smell nice. There's no ulterior motive, for humans anyway."

"Yes," said Marvin.

"A tree gives shade as part of its being. There's no ulterior motive, no obligation."

"I know, Father."

"If you see a starving person and you give him food, there's no ulterior motive. What can he give you back? But when you give something and want something in return ..."

"I don't understand, Father."

"I'm saying this: it isn't going to make me feel any different about your music if you never gave me a dime, or even if you gave me a million dollars. You cannot change me. When ..."

"But I'm not trying to."

"When I became a minister I swore to a poverty life. I don't want to be rich. I don't want my reward here on earth. I will get mine in the spiritual world."

"But, Father, it isn't what you think. It's not like that at all."

Father didn't want to listen. He waved Marvin off and went back to his room.

Marvin once told me that love doesn't require anything back. That's all he wanted from Father. That and a hug.

7

"Why would I screw things up by cattin' around?" Marvin protested. "I would never even think of doing that."

"C'mon, Bro, you're talking to me."

There was a short pause on the line. "Well, I might think about it, but I'd never touch nobody. Nobody, honest."

That's how Marvin reacted to my question about him playing around on Anna. I'd heard the rumors. Most everybody did, including Anna. What brought it all to a head was the announcement that they were getting married. Not a great way to start off, but Anna must have believed his denials. I wanted to believe him too, because I wanted him to settle down.

Marvin loved Anna deeply, but I also knew about the times he had chances to cheat on her. He had told me about the ladies in the office, even the ladies who sang for Motown. "Everybody was making it," he had said. He had also told me about the young girls who swarmed around him after the shows, even offered themselves to him, but he never went any further than that in the things he said. Knowing Marvin as I did and how he loved to tell all, down to the juiciest details, after he'd hooked up with someone, I'm sure he would have said something. He told me he wasn't playing around, so I was sure he was telling the truth when he put down the rumors. We had no secrets.

Anna and Marvin were married in June 1963. The wedding and reception took place in Detroit, and were attended by his adopted Motown family. His real family in D.C. was absent on purpose. Marvin didn't want his two families to mix, not at that time, anyway.

To show his love for Anna, Marvin had written a song with Norman Whitfield and Mickey Stevenson called "Pride and Joy," which had been released on an album earlier in the year. The song was such a success—it reached No. 2 on the R&B charts and crossed over to make the pop Top Ten—that it was re-released as a single only shortly before the wedding. "Pride and Joy" not only made an impression on Anna, it made an impression on the public, too, who turned Marvin into Motown's biggest solo artist.

Marvin was on a roll. He had more hit singles, including the gospel-based "Can I Get a Witness" and more songs for Anna: "You're a Wonderful One" and "How Sweet It Is (To Be Loved by You)." He took a promotional trip to England to establish himself there. He had top billing with the latest Motown Revue, higher than Little Stevie, the Supremes, even Smokey Robinson. And he got an offer to play the lead in *The Sam Cooke Story,* a proposed movie biography of his early singing idol, who had only recently been killed. (Of the movie role, which Marvin turned down, he said, nervous at the thought, "Imagine me *acting* and *singing,* in front of all those cameras and Hollywood people. I can hardly get up the nerve to stand on a stage. Besides, Sam was one of the great singers of all time. I wouldn't do him right.")

Even with so much going on, Marvin also had his own touring show, the Marvin Gaye Revue, which took him to several major US cities, including Detroit, where he played the Twenty Grand Club. Backed by the Spinners and a ten-piece orchestra, the Revue was a huge hit and broke attendance records at more than one stop along the way. Said one reviewer, "The show could turn out to be one of the greatest shows of the year. The versatile singer, Marvin Gaye, and his Revue, left the audience begging for more." Marvin got to sing his hits, as well as a few standards, which pleased everyone, including the reviewer, who added, "He has a way with a ballad that will push him out of the rock 'n' roll category one of these days, and then it will be the posh supper clubs for Mr. Gaye. But whether it is ballads or blues, Marv's timing and phrasing are flawless. The more you hear of him the more you want to hear."

Marvin must have read the review. When he appeared at Bimbo's, in San Francisco, his act had been completely revamped. On his own for these engagements, he basically changed everything, top to bottom, from his selections to his appearance onstage. Marvin said he was "a sensation." He should have said "an immediate sensation," because the initial reaction of his fans when they caught sight of him was lots of whooping and hollering. They were even jamming and jumping as he broke into his opening number, but after that they calmed down, not quite sure what was happening in front of them. For one thing, Marvin was in one of his lovey-dovey moods. He strolled out looking so suave in a top hat and tails, of all things, acting like Romeo but coming across as the Dapper Dans in 1930s movie musicals. It wasn't a great look for him, even though he oozed cool; still, Marvin was made for the ladies, and he knew it.

Then there were the songs. He changed them too, doing more old standards, slow ballads. "They were for Anna," he said. "I was singing to her, but all the ladies thought I was singing to them." Most performers know that to get an audience going, you open with an uptempo number. Not Marvin. He had to do things his way. He was Sinatra, looking like Astaire. He even attempted a few dance steps— with his two left feet. The fans didn't get it, or if they did, they didn't want it. He was convinced he had given them the greatest show on earth.

Marvin got a far different reaction when he started doing the same act, dressed in top hat and tails, in the smart supper clubs. At New York's swank Copacabana and others, the crowds loved his singing the romantic songs in his clear, pure voice. Marvin could caress a song like no other singer. He could even bring tears to the eyes of the upper crust.

Despite his positive reception, singing before live audiences, even in intimate nightclubs, really wasn't Marvin's thing. He liked the atmosphere and the attention, but he wanted to get home to Anna. She was expecting a baby, he told me, but he wouldn't say when. "It's a fact, Bro," he gushed. "She's even starting to show. You're going to be an uncle."

I loved the sound of that, and the excitement in Marvin's voice.

"What about you?" he asked. "'Bout time you hooked up and made me proud."

"What are you talking about?"

"You ... getting hitched and having kids."

"Yeah, well, that'll happen when it's time. It's your time now, and I'm real happy for you and Anna."

"We're thrilled, too, Bro. But do me a favor."

"What's that, Marvin?"

"Hold off on telling Mother and Father ... for a while, anyway ... just to be safe."

"What do you mean?"

"Well, it's happening, but it's still early, so you never know. Just wait, that's all."

I told him I would, but the family eventually heard the news. Unlike Father, who kept his mouth shut on the subject, Mother anxiously looked forward to the big day. She knew how much Marvin had wanted a child. He absolutely loved children, and had longed for one of his own. Once the secret was out, Marvin openly talked with Mother about the coming event. He was completely up-front with her about his excitement, and with all of us at home, as well as with his friends and coworkers in Detroit—even with the press. There was only one thing he kept to himself. Anna wasn't pregnant; she couldn't have children, which neither Anna nor Marvin wanted anyone to know. When Marvin told me Anna was "starting to show," it was only because she had purposely gained weight to throw everyone off.

Marvin knew what was going on all along, but he didn't want to share any of it, even after little Marvin was born. Even then he began to tell people that the baby was adopted, though the truth was more complicated than that.

The truth, which he eventually told Mother, was that in order to strengthen their marriage, Marvin and Anna decided to have a child in a pretty unusual kind of way. Anna was growing increasingly jealous over her twenty-six-year-old husband, who always seemed to be surrounded and pursued by beautiful young women. They flocked around him wherever he went, and his romantic duets with Mary Wells and Kim Weston on records didn't help. Much of it was publicity, but at forty-two, Anna believed the reports. Her insecurities only made things worse, Marvin said. They fought, not only at home, but often when they were in public. They still loved each other and needed each other, but something was missing. A baby was what they needed to pull them closer together again.

Rumors swirled about who really had the baby. There was even talk that Anna got Marvin together with one of her younger relations, just to keep it in the Gordy family. I'm sure Marvin told Mother who really carried the baby, but she didn't tell me, and I didn't ask. I really didn't want to know. Marvin and Anna had their baby, and that was all that mattered to me.

Marvin Pentz Gaye, III, was born in November 1965. None of Marvin's real family was at the hospital or even at the christening. Maxine Powell, the lady who ran Motown's charm school, was named the baby's godmother.

"Did I hear you right?" I asked Marvin, once I heard the baby's name. "Is that really what you're calling the boy?"

"I know, I know," he said, almost apologetically, "but I had to do it. He's my father, and you know I love him, at some times more than at other times, but I do love him. Besides, it's tradition. We learned that in the Bible."

"We did?" I said.

"Yes, we did," he replied. "Weren't you paying attention?"

"Always," I answered. Then we both had a good laugh.

Little Marvin brought Marvin and Anna closer than they had been since the earliest days of their marriage. Marvin worshipped the boy, and from all I heard, Anna loved him as if he were her own natural-born son. Still, according to Marvin, there came a time when the old tensions began to return. Much of it was Berry Gordy's doing. The success of Marvin's recorded duets with Mary Wells and Kim Weston had people talking. Marvin and Mary Wells hit with the single "What's the Matter with You, Baby" and the album *Together,* which included such romantic ballads as "Until I Met You," "(I Love You) For Sentimental Reasons," "After the Lights Go Down Low," and "Squeeze Me." Kim Weston and Marvin enchanted the public with such singles as "I Want You 'Round" and "It Takes Two," and with the album *Take Two,* and its multiple hits. In his duets with both women, the voices captured a sound and an emotion—a real clicking—that it seemed to audiences could never have happened only in moments in front of a microphone. There had to be something going on between the singers. The public believed it was listening to recorded love affairs. Anna was never sure about what was going on.

"Nothing!" Marvin kept insisting, denying all the talk. "There's nothing between any of us. It's all in everyone's minds. They want to believe what they believe. I love them both, but not in that way."

Mary Wells denied it, too. So did Kim Weston. "We had a brother-sister relationship," she has said. "The love I had for him wasn't like the love of a lover. It was a more genuine love. Besides, I was in love with somebody else at the time. Mickey Stevenson and I were getting married."

The controversy proved commercially successful for Motown, and a dream come true for the gossip columnists. For Marvin it was altogether different. "It's screwing up my mind," he said uneasily. "They've made me into a sex symbol. How can any man live up to that?"

It would get worse. Hanging around the Motown offices, putting in her time and waiting her turn, just like most everyone else had done, was a bright, talented, and extremely attractive young lady, barely twenty-one, named Tammi Terrell. As a teenager, she had been part of James Brown's revue, using her real name, Tammi Montgomery.

Mary Wells had left Motown and Kim Weston was leaving to get married. Now Berry brought Marvin and Tammi together, and they hit it off immediately. Said Marvin, "I wanted to work with Tammi. She was so beautiful, warm, sweet, and soft. I rehearsed with her and really dug her voice ... it seemed to fit in with my style just right. We had a great chemistry together, which made it sound like we were lovers. We truly were, but only in the recording studio." Marvin couldn't understand why Anna was jealous of Tammi. She knew that Tammi was in love with David Ruffin, a member of the Temptations. Marvin said everyone knew that.

Tammi and Marvin recorded their first single—a song by Motown's new songwriting team, Nickolas Ashford and Valerie Simpson—in December 1966. That song, "Ain't No Mountain High Enough," turned out to be such a huge hit that Motown sent Marvin and Tammi off on tour. "We had a blast together," said Marvin.

Having Marvin on the road with Tammi, and knowing how close the two could get during their performances, did not sit well with Anna. She accused Marvin of playing around, which he swore was not true, so he in turn accused her of doing the same thing while he was away. Lots of mean-spirited words were tossed around, plus a few objects, during their heated arguments. It didn't seem to matter that little Marvin was around.

While Anna and Marvin's marriage became increasingly strained, America had its own problems. The country was involved in a war in Vietnam that split the nation. The most vocal young generation in history began to wage its own war against the Establishment. Riots were turning cities into mini–war zones, and once peaceful college campuses, where students staged antiwar demonstrations, became scenes of upheaval and gunfire. It was a confusing time, one that had Marvin growing frustrated. His rebellious nature had him wanting to express himself through his songs, but that was impossible at Motown, where political themes were vetoed in favor of love in its various stages and tempos, from discovery and lustful yearning to loneliness and rejection. So Marvin kept recording his bouncy love songs and working with the songwriters in residence, who were trying to come up with hits that were offensive to no one.

They hit it big from time to time, too. One of Marvin's co-authored songs, "Dancing in the Street," became a Motown classic. Originally a big hit for Martha and the Vandellas, it has been brought back over the years by the Mamas and the Papas (1967), Van Halen (1982), and Mick Jagger and David Bowie (1985).

I once asked Marvin how he liked swallowing his ego, knowing how he liked doing things his own way. "It all depends on how much you want to get something done," he said. "Berry takes all the credit for everything, anyway." From the way he talked, he was simply marking time. He had a plan, he said, but it hadn't taken shape yet. He'd make his move when the inspiration hit him.

To me, living faraway in drab D.C., Marvin's life sounded so glamorous. I had no ambition to be a songwriter, so hearing about the controlling inner workings at Motown didn't discourage me. I wanted only to be a professional singer, like my brother. We had grown up singing, and his success made me want it even more. Marvin knew that, but the way we sounded, the way we looked, so much the same, made me feel that wasn't going to happen. I knew I could get singing jobs, but the more famous Marvin became, the more people would think I was riding his coattails, taking advantage of his celebrity. How could I make a name for myself? I would always be known as Marvin Gaye's little brother. It was that way already, wherever I went.

It's true that Marvin only halfheartedly encouraged me to sing at that time. Whether it was sibling rivalry, as some writers have assumed, or because he wanted to protect me from the unsavory aspects of the music business, I don't know. I truly feel he didn't want me to get hurt. When we were children, Marvin had always been protective of me. He may have gotten me in trouble at home with his pranks, but that was kids' play, fun stuff. As adults, he remained protective—as much as he could. In Detroit, and on the road, he couldn't watch me but he called a lot to make sure everything was okay. If I wasn't making enough money at whatever odd job I was doing, even when I worked as a doorman at one of the D.C. hotels, he always made sure I was taken care of. There came a time, however, when he simply couldn't protect me any longer. In early 1967, I was drafted and sent to fight in Vietnam.

Halfway across the world, thousands of miles from home, living among strangers, made me uneasy for a while. Then letters began coming and I heard Marvin's voice on the Armed Forces Radio Network, which never tired of playing his music. Despite my surroundings, I felt a real connection to the people and places at home. "I'm one of the lucky ones," I told myself whenever I heard Marvin's voice. He may have been singing over a transistor radio in the next bunk, the next room, or over a loudspeaker somewhere, but he was there, with me. It seemed nothing could pull us apart.

Between September 1967 and November 1969, Marvin was at his commercial peak. He chalked up one major R&B hit after another, an average of one every two months. The majority of them were duets with Tammi Terrell, songs like "You Got What It Takes," "Your Precious Love," "You're All I Need to Get By," "If I Could Build My Whole World Around You," and "Ain't Nothing Like the Real Thing." When I first heard many of those songs I didn't know that they had all been recorded before the summer of 1967. And it wasn't until months after that I learned, in a letter from Marvin, that Tammi had collapsed in his arms on the stage of Virginia's Hampton-Sydney College during a performance. Marvin wrote, "All of a sudden, while we were singing 'Your Precious Love,' she stopped and fell against me. I thought she had just fainted, as I held her and carried her offstage, but it was worse than that. We still don't know what really happened to her or what's wrong with her, but she's so sick. It just isn't right. It's like all love has gone out of my heart."

Marvin had always tried to be upbeat whenever he wrote to me, knowing where I was and all that was going on around me. But his letters took on a different, darker tone after that. I knew how much he truly cared for Tammi, and I prayed for her recovery.

Over the next months Marvin fed me bits of news about Tammi's condition, and none of it was encouraging. He told me about the headaches she'd had, and ignored, before her collapse. He wrote about a possible brain tumor, brain surgery, her weight loss, and her partial paralysis. There were rumors that her boyfriend, David Ruffin, had hit her on the head, causing her current problems.

It wasn't until years later that Kim Weston told me that Ruffin was not to blame. Kim said, "It definitely wasn't David Ruffin. I will not name the person, but Tammi personally told me it was a very famous artist who kicked her in the head and down a flight of stairs, which resulted in her having a plate put in her head. This is what Tammi told me, and it happened before she came to Motown, before she even knew David Ruffin."

Marvin dwelled on Tammi for months; he even wrote of taking a break from singing, maybe even disappearing from show business for a while. Then he had some positive news, but it was long in coming. Before I had left for Vietnam, Marvin had told me about a song he'd recorded called "I Heard It Through the Grapevine." He loved the production—everything, that is, except his performance. He felt he wasn't into the song during the session, and that he really hadn't come into himself yet as an artist. "I could have done so much better," he admitted. Berry Gordy must have felt the same way because he put a hold on the record's release. As I understand it, Norman Whitfield, who had cowritten "Grapevine" with Barrett Strong, felt so strongly about Marvin's recording that he began hounding Berry to release it. Berry wouldn't. Instead, he agreed to give the song to another artist just to get Norman off his back.

"Grapevine" was given to Gladys Knight and the Pips, her backup singers consisting of her brother Merald (Bubba) and cousins Edward Patten and William Guest. Their rousing version, with Gladys's strong gospel lead voice, was released in September 1967, and became the group's first hit, selling over two million copies. Even

Marvin, disappointed that it wasn't his version, had to admit that Gladys's recording was sensational. "Gladys and the Pips did a great job, and they deserved hitting No. 1 with it." (No. 1 on the R&B charts, and No. 2 on the pop charts.)

According to Marvin, Norm Whitfield never gave up on getting Marvin's recording released. "It has a totally different sound," he told Berry. "It has 'hit single' written all over it." Again, Berry turned him down. Norman had won the first time around with Berry—not with Marvin's recording, but he got the song out—and it made Berry look good, so he kept pressing, this time to include it in Marvin's next album. Now that the song had big-time recognition, he knew it would help sell the album. Berry finally gave in.

Marvin's album *I Heard It Through the Grapevine* was released in August 1968, almost simultaneously with his second album of duets with Tammi, *You're All I Need*. It was Marvin's version of "Grapevine" that dominated airplay, so much so that Motown released the song as a single two months later. Just as Gladys's version with the Pips reached No. 1, so did Marvin's. In fact, it became not only Marvin's first No. 1 pop single, but Motown's too—and it topped the charts for nearly two months.

Marvin's letters kept coming, and they were always filled with welcome news about home and his career, but not all the happenings were positive. At one point he wrote about the ongoing civil unrest in the States. There were problems in Watts, in Chicago, at Kent State in Ohio, and even in Detroit, where looting and rioting had left part of the city in flames. "Armed National Guardsmen came," he said, "as well as part of the Army. Those guys were all over. We heard gunfire out on the streets, so it got pretty close. I pray for the people everywhere, and especially for you. Be strong, Frankie, we're all with you."

We had heard via the Armed Forces Radio Network about the assassinations of Robert F. Kennedy and the Reverend Dr. Martin Luther King, both shot down in the same year, 1968. Everyone in my outfit was wondering what was going on in the world. So much killing, so much hatred. Marvin wondered too.

Around the time of Dr. King's death, Marvin wrote that he had taken part in a weeklong series of variety shows, put on by Quincy Jones and members of the Institute for Black American Music, to raise funds for civil rights causes. The shows were held at the Chicago Amphitheater and featured one of the greatest all-star casts ever put together. All the Motown artists were there, he wrote, along with Flip Wilson; Dick Gregory; Richard Pryor; Sammy Davis, Jr.; Bill Cosby; and the cast of "Sesame Street." Marvin noted, "With so many people around doing their thing, I was only a small part of the show. I wanted to do more, but I was glad to be there doing whatever they needed me to do." He also added, "Wish you could have seen the faces when I came out with my new look. I shaved my head to show my support of the protests." He didn't say exactly what he was protesting, but I later learned it was the imprisonment of Rubin "Hurricane" Carter.

Marvin loved being with Quincy Jones—working with him and learning from him. "He has so much talent," Marvin wrote. "You want to be involved in everything he does. Marvin had the bright idea of collaborating with Quincy on one of his albums, but the only response he got from Motown was no; they thought Quincy was too "jazzy" for their artists. What a team Quincy and Marvin would have made.

The last letter I got from Marvin in Vietnam arrived only days before I was to ship out for my return home. I had been away a long time. Now I was counting down to ETS, our abbreviation for what we called the Estimated Time to Split—the big day—and I could hardly wait to see my family again. Marvin said he would try to be in D.C. to welcome me, but I had my doubts. This was Marvin's darkest letter of all. He sounded totally lost.

It wasn't Motown that would keep Marvin in Detroit. Berry Gordy was thinking of moving Motown to Hollywood, Marvin said. "Who knows when, but just the thought of leaving has put a bad taste in the mouths of everyone he'd be leaving behind. There are also the folks who feel he'd be deserting the city, and them." Actually,

Berry wanted to make the move to be with his favorite Supreme, his lover, Diana Ross, whose solo career he was pushing. Movies as well as recordings were in his plans for Diana, and Hollywood was where he could mastermind both. "I'm not following him," Marvin wrote, "I've had enough of that."

It wasn't Anna either, he noted. One day he loved her, the next day he didn't. Their relationship ran hot and cold, but was growing more cold than hot. They fought, then made up, then fought some more, which didn't make for the best of times. They went for long periods without ever seeing each other; Marvin was good at disappearing.

It was probably a combination of things that had Marvin so low, but I suspected it was the last thing he mentioned because he said so little about it. Just telling me must have been difficult for him. I know it filled his head and hurt his heart just trying to get it out. All he said was, "Tammi died yesterday." That was it. His letter was dated March 17th, 1970.

———

"WELCOME HOME, FRANKIE!" A big paper banner was tacked over the front door at home. Standing there, seeing it, I thought I'd melt down, but I was saved when the screen door popped open and Mother came running out. Then came Father and Sweetsie. No Jeanne, no Marvin, I told myself.

I felt smothered in the warmth from the hugs and kisses that I received from Mother and Sweetsie. Father stayed off to the side, taking it all in and smiling. I know I looked like a fool, trying to act brave with tears streaming down my cheeks, but I was finally home with my family and it didn't matter. I didn't have to be brave anymore.

Marvin was up to his old tricks, just like when we were kids. He was behind Mother, stooping down, just about bursting to keep from busting out with laughter. I was so happy to see him he could have been standing on his head for all I cared.

Marvin was glad to be home too, to get away from everything in Detroit for a while, and to feel family again. There were times when things got a little awkward so we had to watch our words. For one thing, we didn't want to bring up sore subjects when Father was around. At the dinner table there could be no talk about Marvin's career, the songs he was writing, his hit records, the cities and countries he had visited and, especially, his sexy image. That was fine with Marvin. There was too much stuff on his mind that he needed to push aside at that time.

Nights were the best, and Marvin and I truly became kids again as we stretched out in our beds, telling stories in the dark. Only now, Marvin wanted me to do the talking. He was full of questions, and they all had to do with my experiences in Vietnam. He wanted to hear everything—what I saw, what I heard, what I felt. I couldn't tell it all in one night—not even in two or three, not with all his questioning—it went on night after night, for over a week.

It wasn't easy for me to give Marvin what he wanted. Until you've fought in a firefight, there is no way you can imagine one, and as I readjusted to civilian life, or tried to, the last thing I wanted to do was relive my war.

"C'mon, Frankie," he'd say, "Talk to me. Tell me."

At first, I played with him. "Watch the news," I told him. "Or buy some comic books. There's a bunch of them that have heroes fighting the Cong." That didn't work, not with Marvin. I should have known it wouldn't. When he wanted something, he usually got it. He wore me down, he wore me out. Finally, I gave in. "Okay, I'll tell you what you want to hear. Where should I start?"

"At the beginning," he said. "Tell me everything."

"Well, first there was basic training."

"And they got you on your name, right?"

"The first day. I knew it was coming, but there was nothing I could do about it. We were all lined up for roll call and some sergeant was barking out the names. When he got to mine there was a long pause, then he squinted his eyes, looked around and hollered, 'Who's Gaye?' My heart was beating like bongos, but I knew I had to respond, so I took a deep breath and, in my deepest voice, I barked out,

'I am, sir.' I got all messed up. I should have said, 'Here, sir.' All the guys laughed and looked at me until the sergeant called them to attention again. I thought I was in for it after that. I did get some ribbing for a while, but all I had to do was mention your name. That got me some respect."

"What happened next?"

"Our orders came in the dead of night and we shipped out. There were 19,000 men packed on the ship and only 5,000 lifeboats. We wondered what would happen to us if we went down. Probably panic and scrambling, with most of us ending up as fish food. If we'd known what was coming, that would have been the easy way out."

"Tell me more," Marvin said.

"It took us 19 days to cross the ocean. I knew it was going to be a long, boring time so I brought something to occupy myself."

"What?"

"A book."

"You read a book?"

"It was a novel called *Strangers When We Meet*. That was the first novel I'd ever read all the way through, and I'm glad I thought ahead. I got so wrapped up in the story I lost track of time."

"Then?"

"Then we saw the coastline of Vietnam and we transferred to the landing crafts. In the darkness we could see bombs going off in the distance and flares exploding high in the night sky. As we got closer to the shore there was nothing to see on land except strange lights that flickered like the bright eyes of monsters. Then somebody shouted. We hit the sand, and ramps crashed down in the shallow water. The landing crafts hit the beach, one after another, and I felt myself being pushed forward. I thought of all the war movies I'd seen and how half the guys never made it onto the beach because the shells would get them while they were still in the water."

Marvin sat up in bed. Leaning against the headboard, he drew up his knees, crossed his arms over them, and lowered his head. "Go on," he said, quietly.

"I have to tell you Marvin, after the way you talked when you got out of the service, I tried hard not to go in. I gave the draft board every excuse I could think of, and that's probably why I wound up in Vietnam. It wasn't that I didn't want to defend my country, I definitely did. But I didn't want to kill anybody. I didn't want to be trapped in a trench with somebody trying to kill me. I didn't want to be sloshing down some stinking river up to my shoulders in murky water with things crawling all over me. I didn't want to see dead people or living people all blown up. I didn't want to be asking questions like 'Why am I here?' But after a while, we all asked ourselves that question. Nobody had the answer."

"More," said Marvin.

"I saw all the things I never wanted to see, and I was in places I never wanted to be. The jungles were so thick and dense that it was permanent midnight for long stretches. You couldn't stand up; you had to crawl through the mud over things that moved when you touched them. It rained so much that everything on the ground rotted and smelled like week-old garbage, from the heat, rain, and humidity. It was often so dark or so steamy that it did no good to look up to see if the enemy was behind the next tree trunk or maybe crouched in front of you. We were so covered with mud it was impossible to identify uniforms or faces. Once you see people dying, cut up, or being tortured, day after day of that, you get desensitized, then paranoid. You think something's always going to happen, even talk yourself into not trusting anyone or anything. Still, you want to believe that there's a reason for what's happening and that good will come of it."

Lying in the dark with Marvin and talking about killing and atrocities, about lost and abandoned children, about all the injustices, there were times when I felt I couldn't continue. It had been some months since I'd been in Vietnam, but in the retelling it felt like yesterday. It was then that he would reach over and hold me in his arms. Then we'd cry on each other's shoulders. The next evening we'd start in again.

One night, after almost a week of questioning, Marvin asked, "Tell me about some of the men you met. What kind of prejudice was there?"

"There was one guy in particular," I said. "He was from the Deep South and he didn't want to be in the same tent with a black man. I thought, 'Here we go again,' when I heard that. Over there, in Vietnam, you really had to leave that at home because those of us who were there, the Americans, had to look out for each other."

I told Marvin that when the guy—his name was Calvin—first moved into the tent he draped a big rebel flag over his footlocker, right in everyone's face. Not a smart move, because we each had a rifle with a bayonet.

When my friend Johnson, who was black, heard about Calvin, he wanted to hurt him. So did the other blacks in the outfit, and some of the whites too. Johnson confronted Calvin about the flag, but he held his ground. He had been taught to feel the way he did. Giving in would have gone against his culture.

When word reached one of the officers, Calvin was ordered to get rid of the flag or sleep outside the tent. Calvin moved out. As much as Calvin disliked me, I felt I had to talk with him, if he could stand being in my company for a while. He wasn't too happy about that but he didn't want any more problems with the higher-ups. "I may be different," I told Calvin, "but so are you. We're all different, and that's what makes each of us special."

"Yeah, but I'm better," Calvin said.

"In what way?" I asked.

"I'm white and you're black."

"The color of your skin doesn't make you better or worse. So what makes you better?"

"What can I tell you? I just am."

"Is it my hair, my IQ? Is that it? What if my IQ is higher than yours?"

He laughed.

"I've done nothing to you, but you look down on me. What makes me inferior to you?"

"Quit messing with me."

"Aren't there some blacks in sports, music, movies, or whatever, that you like, maybe even look up to once in a while? Women and men who have made a name for themselves in their professions?"

"Maybe."

"Do you know what those people had to go through to get where they are? How did Jackie Robinson do it? How did the players that followed him do it? How did they stand in front of all those people, take the calls from the umpires and the boos from the crowds and still focus on hitting the ball? They already had a strike or two against them, so they had to be better than the rest of the best."

Marvin looked at me intently and asked, "What did Calvin say to that?"

"He didn't say anything. He just sat quietly, staring at the ground. And then I told him about you."

"Me?" Marvin said.

"How you've had to deal with our name and the things that have happened on the road, not only to you, but to every black entertainer. I told him about Sammy Davis, Jr., and how he couldn't stay at the same hotel with Sinatra and the rest of his clan, or even walk through the front door, until Sinatra threatened to pull the Rat Pack stars offstage and cancel the engagement. Name a black entertainer who doesn't have horror stories to tell. Then they have to stand in the spotlight and sing happy songs, tell jokes, or do whatever they do, and make their paying audiences feel like they've seen something special. That takes not only talent but real strength, and guts."

"Did you tell Calvin about Father?" Marvin asked.

"No, I didn't want to get into religion. He could have gone off on another wild tear with that. But I must have said something that touched a nerve because Calvin was different after we got together. He told me nobody had ever told him any of that stuff. All he knew was what his parents had told him."

"But he still slept outside, right?"

"He moved back inside and we wound up not just friends, but good friends. He even invited me to visit him when we got out. He actually wanted to take me to his home."

"What did you say to that?" asked Marvin.

"I told him that wasn't a good idea. His parents would probably have flipped out if they saw me coming. So I told him to talk with his parents and go slow with them. He may not succeed with them but I have hope for his kids, the new generation, when it comes along."

Marvin was tiring, but he still wanted to hear more. There really wasn't much left to tell him, only about my scheduled day of departure from Vietnam, that long-awaited day. "We were all at the airport in Saigon, hundreds of us, without weapons, ready to head home. We should have been in a good mood, but we weren't. Everything we'd collected and saved as souvenirs or gifts to bring home, basically anything made of metal, was taken away from us, yanked away from us. Small thing, I guess, considering all we'd been through. New troops, all green guys, were arriving; it was like they'd emptied the jails, to see all the new meat coming in. Then, without warning, we were back in the war. The airport in Saigon was being bombarded with mortar shells, from five miles away. The new troops panicked and started shooting at anything that moved. Bodies were dropping in every direction. Before the attack I had seen one of the guys I had known back at camp writing home as he waited to leave. Next time I looked he was on the ground, his letter soaked in blood. He had already done his tour of duty, and now it was really over for him. 'Oh, Lord,' I prayed, running behind a barrier of sand bags, 'don't let anything more happen. Get us home ... get us all home.' Another ten minutes passed before we heard the all-clear signal."

Marvin was quiet at first as he sat propped up in bed, his face buried in his hands. When he finally spoke, his words came out slowly. In his soft voice he said, "I didn't know how to fight before, but now I think I do. I just have to do it my way. I'm not a painter, I'm not a poet. But I can do it with music."

8

The political and cultural upheaval that flamed through America at the end of the '60s did not pass Motown by. In a reflection of the times, Berry Gordy found his music empire slowly disintegrating, as many of the artists he had discovered and turned into stars began defecting. Leaving the label were Gladys Knight and the Pips, the Isley Brothers, the Spinners, the Four Tops, and even the hit-making creative team of Holland–Dozier–Holland.

Marvin, too, considered cutting ties with Motown, but several factors kept him from bolting. Although his marriage to Anna was growing shakier by the day, he still cared deeply for her, and he always would. What made their relationship especially difficult had nothing to do with Anna's jealous rages or her constant charges that he was cheating. While he certainly had his chances to be unfaithful to Anna, Marvin always swore his innocence. "I have never cheated on her," Marvin would say over and over. "I have never played around." The tables turned, however, when Marvin returned to Detroit following my big welcome home. Marvin caught Anna cheating. "I came home early one night and Anna wasn't there," he told me. "Something inside made me suspicious, so I got in my car and drove around until I found myself turning the car into a motel parking lot. I had no idea why I stopped there, but there was a pull that made me turn in, like I was a hunk of metal being drawn along by a magnet.

"Finding the room was the same thing. I'd never been to that room; I'd never even been to that motel at all, but when I got to the door and opened it, there she was. I was blown away. What made me go to that place? What made *her* go to that place? No one had said anything to me about Anna fooling around. I had no clue. It was almost like she wanted me to find her."

I could only imagine how Marvin felt. Life with the two of them may have been rough before, but it was nothing compared to what it was like after that. Not much later she threw her expensive wedding ring into the backyard of their home. Another time, she took a razor blade to Marvin's five-hundred-dollar suits. To get even, he torched her fur coats. "Man, what have I gotten myself into?" he moaned.

Marvin's feelings for Anna's brother weren't especially raves either, but a certain loyalty remained for the man who had basically molded his career. More than anything, however, Marvin was influenced by memories of his childhood. From where we had lived as youngsters, it was possible to see the domes and rooftops of various government buildings in the distance. We knew the power and wealth that existed just outside our own backyard, while at the same time, we were immediately surrounded by poverty and despair.

Marvin knew that his interests might be better served if he, too, were to cut his ties with Motown, but he also believed—to put it bluntly—that the interests of his own people could only be furthered if black stayed with black. For Marvin to have signed with another record label (and he was being secretly courted at the time) would not only be betraying Berry, it would be betraying his own people. He could not do that.

That was Marvin's decision, despite the incredible injustices that Motown was heaping upon him; it was a decision that also came with an idea. The nightlong discussions that Marvin and I had had about

Vietnam were taking musical shape in his mind, songs and themes like no others he had ever written or recorded before. Included, too, in his thoughts was a song he had heard several months earlier called "What's Going On." Al Cleveland, who had written the piece with Renaldo Benson of the Four Tops, had brought it to Marvin, wanting him to record it. At the time, Marvin liked what he heard, but he wasn't sure it was right for him. A good song, a beautiful song, but controversial—maybe too controversial, like the Temptations' recording of the protest song, "Ball of Confusion," written by Norm Whitfield and Barrett Strong.

Although Marvin had wanted to pass "What's Going On" along to another artist when Al first brought it to him, he began to have second thoughts. The song's strong message fit in perfectly with his own concerns about world problems. He had found a new creative approach and his fight was on.

According to Marvin, "We went into the studio and cut a tape, which came out really good. With the right handling I knew it could make an impact. But Berry only wanted to mess with me. He had to know how the song came to be, who wrote it, why I hadn't wanted to record it at first. He picked up on the fact that I hadn't written it, but felt I should get a piece of it, at least some credit since I'd brought my voice to the recording and had felt so strongly about it to take it this far. I told him Al and Renaldo had agreed to let me share the credit. He nodded, then started sticking it to them and me, saying how he was worried about me hanging out with hippies who were lazy and had it in for the government. Before he could say any more, I told him he'd better hear the song first."

Before starting the tape, Marvin explained to Berry how he had brought his friends from the Detroit Lions, Mel Farr and Lem Barney, to add their voices to the opening seconds of the party sounds. Then he started the tape. "Hey, what's happening? Good party, man. Dig it." The background chatter and clatter soon gave way to a driving Motown beat. Berry smiled and started moving to the catchy tempo. "Mother, mother, there's too many of you crying." Hearing that, and all else that followed, Berry's expression froze. "You've got to be kidding," he said. "Nobody will buy this garbage."

"I didn't know what to do," Marvin said later. "One minute he was all smiles, talking monster hit. The next he was exploding, shouting 'trash music,' and telling me to get my head on straight. Damn Berry Gordy. He doesn't like 'What's Going On'? Wait till he hears everything else I have to say!"

Marvin would not be discouraged. In fact, Berry's put-down only motivated him more. He loved going against the grain, and now his goal to make a meaningful sociological statement—and still sell records—was filled with even more passion.

Marvin went into a zone. He became isolated, a man in a bubble, writing furiously, mainly alone but sometimes with others who shared his musical vision. It seemed almost sinful to interrupt him with a phone call. We often held off, waiting for him to call.

How could he keep up the pace, we wondered. How could he keep going under the pressures he had set for himself? "God is writing the album," he would say. "I sit at the piano and music comes out, flowing from God." Mother worried about him, his friends worried about him, as the summer of 1970 turned into fall. He was still writing and making demos. Every once in a while he'd let me listen to a new song or two. My introduction to his new album was over the phone, hearing songs about all sorts of societal problems: "Mercy Mercy Me (The Ecology)" addressed the environment and pollution. He brought the plight of the poor painfully to life in "Inner City Blues (Make Me Wanna Holler)," and "Save the Children" was aimed at getting people to pay attention to the whole future of the world. There was one song he refused to play for me. "I'll send you a tape," he said. "Listen carefully."

The tape he sent was "What's Happening, Brother." The title threw me, and as I listened to the words, I couldn't believe what I was hearing. Marvin, my brother, the star, was so inspired by me that he had written a song about me—for me—a song about the frustrations of a returning Vietnam vet, a song that was so personal and heartfelt I started to cry. I cried every time I played it because I knew what it took for Marvin to write that song. I cried because I was so proud of him for all the songs in the album, and for standing up for his beliefs—and voicing them.

Not many days later I saw some photos of Marvin in one of the papers. I hardly recognized him with his beard, a beard like mine, and the clothes he wore. Gone were the fashionable, Dapper Dan duds, the suave outfits required by the Motown dress code. Now he wore sweat suits and sneakers. He had taken on my baggy, casual image. According to the caption, "His new look surprised some of his fans and pleased others, who claimed he looked even sexier."

At one point during his stretch of songwriting, Marvin took a break to do interviews in Chicago, where he made some highly publicized remarks in support of the Black Panthers and the Black Power movement. Marvin loved the Panthers even though he never completely agreed with their policies. "What I like, I really like," he admitted. "The brothers need waking up because so many of us are being killed and hurt. There's no need for the beatings and shootings that go on in the inner city. And too many of our people are homeless and going hungry. The Panthers go door-to-door for donations of food or money to help the poor. I support that."

What Marvin didn't support, actually despised, was the Panthers militant and often violent actions, along with their antigovernment stance. Nor could he tolerate what he called "the pig thing," the Panthers' attitude toward the police. We had been brought up to respect the police, not to mess with them. We knew there were things they didn't always do right. Growing up in D.C. we'd seen what had happened to people in the area, kids and grown-ups alike, who'd gone against the law. We knew about the shootings and beatings, but we were taught to believe that the majority of cops were good, and only a few gave them a bad name. "The ones who abuse the badge don't make them all bad," Marvin would say. "Too many people think in terms of stark black-and-white. To me, the world is only shades of gray."

Marvin's remarks didn't please the brass at Motown, who wanted their artists to be squeaky clean and uncontroversial. Nor did they like him carrying books by Malcolm X to interviews, holding them in plain sight. Marvin stood his ground by saying, "I have to be me," which came as no surprise. He had always been too open, too non-conforming. No one could tell him what to do.

The early 1970s have been described as Marvin's political period. Looking back, his entire career was a political statement, but to me it was more the time when he won his independence as a writer, producer, arranger, and performer. Marvin stopped dreaming and started doing.

To his fans, Marvin's reputation as a "stubborn kind of fellow" was simply tied to a song he had recorded early in his career at Motown. But his stubbornness was real, and it reached a new level once he had all the songs for the new album, which he called *What's Going On*. Marvin knew that getting the songs past Berry Gordy wouldn't be easy. Berry had already called the title song "garbage." What would he say about the rest of them, or the album's concept? Motown had never released a concept album before. No other label had either.

"This is totally new," he told Berry to open their meeting. "There's a theme that runs throughout. Some songs run longer than others, even in and out of each other. It's jazz, pop, gospel, R&B, all rolled into one. I know it's not a typical Motown album, but I'm really proud of it."

"You've got this great, sexy image," Berry told him, "and you've got to protect it."

"I don't care about image," Marvin replied. "I just gotta do it. You've gotta let me do it."

Marvin was turned down flat, which had him running to the phone. "Berry hates my music," Marvin said, angrily. "He doesn't want to record it because he doesn't think it will sell. He may be right about that, but I don't care. I just want it to be heard, and that's all that matters."

"How could he not like those songs? They're the best you've ever done." I hoped he could hear the disappointment in my voice.

"I wanted to remind him how he felt about 'Grapevine' at first, and how wrong he was about that one."

"Didn't you?"

"No."

"Does that mean it's not going to happen?"

"Oh, it's gonna happen, all right. I just don't know how, right now."

Marvin hounded Berry Gordy for months, as well as the other decision-makers at Motown, individually and as a unit, during the weekly music-review meetings. "Listen to these songs, he'd tell them. Listen with both ears and hear the songs through. It isn't a bunch of separate songs, like you're used to hearing, it's the musical whole. You've got to listen to get into it."

Tempers flared as the board members waited to see Berry's thumbs-up or, at least, something other than his sour expression. The meetings always ended on a down note. Looking back, Motown was ignoring a trend in the music business at the time. The Vietnam War was the first American war that produced more protest songs than patriotic ones, partly because Vietnam and the civil rights movement were happening all at once. Then there was the folk movement. Rock music of the late 1960s and into the early '70s was moving along the lines of modern folk music.

Marvin would almost always tell us when he was coming home. This time he didn't, and he arrived in a rage. Before he even saw Mother, he was in my room, slamming the door and saying, "That's it, I quit Motown."

"You did what? You're putting me on."

"I told Berry," he said, standing and pacing, "I told all of them, either put out *What's Going On* or I'll never record another note for them again."

"You can't do that," I told him. "You have a contract with them. They can hold you to it. They can sue you."

"They can try," he said, defiantly. "Let them try."

"How many albums are you supposed to turn in every year?"

"Three."

"How many times have you done that since you've been with Motown?"

"Twice, maybe."

"You could owe them ten or 12 albums. They could make things rough for you."

Marvin stopped pacing and looked away. All he could say was, "Oh, man." He came over to the bed and slumped down as if he hadn't a friend in the world, especially in Detroit, which wasn't quite true. Unknown to Marvin, there were other disenchanted creative talents at Motown who were coming over to his side. A few, like Stevie Wonder, who had always hated being labeled "Little Stevie," even when he was a youngster, listened silently. Others— most notably, Smokey Robinson, Diana Ross, David Ruffin, Edwin Starr, and Norm Whitfield—were more vocal in their support of Marvin. Having already lost a number of its top artists to other labels, Motown must have felt the pressure, even the possibility of a black protest, which was gaining strength in parts of America, including Detroit. Much of white America, too, was angry. It seemed the whole country was riled up over events taking place at home and around the world.

In January 1971, much to Marvin's surprise, "What's Going On" was released as a single. Marvin didn't know until it was in the stores. Neither did Berry Gordy. Whoever ordered the release of the record must have felt his wrath, because Marvin said everyone heard the sound of his voice bellowing, "It's the worst record I've ever heard."

Marvin didn't know what to do next. Berry's opinion of the single never wavered, even as it became Motown's fastest-selling single, with over 70,000 copies sold in its first week. "Berry is beside himself," Marvin reported when the record topped the charts at No. 1 and set the rock world spinning. "He's so shaken with the record's success. He had prided himself on knowing the business, and on being able to predict what would sell and what wouldn't."

The single had people all over the country calling radio stations and music stores for Marvin Gaye recordings, anything by Marvin Gaye. Many of them had never heard of Marvin before, simply because his earlier work had been played only on R&B stations. Now he was being heard all over the dials.

Within the month, Motown was demanding an album. "Nothing's ready yet," Marvin replied. "Berry told me to hold off on it because he doesn't think it will sell."

"He what?" was the reply. "When was that?"

"When he heard the demos," said Marvin. "The same time I demoed 'What's Going On' for him." Marvin explained that all the songs for an album were written, but nothing had been studio-recorded.

Marvin was basically told to "get busy," but he had other things on his mind before he would set foot in a studio. If he was to stay at Motown and give the label what it wanted, he had a few requests—or rather, demands—that had to be met.

In March 1971, after a series of sometimes-heated meetings with Berry Gordy and the Motown brass, Marvin stepped into the studio to record the *What's Going On* album, knowing he had won his independence at Motown. From this point on, he would be allowed to record and release what he wanted, as well as to use the musicians, producers, and arrangers of his choice. With his victory, he had rewritten the rules at Motown.

Released in May 1971, the *What's Going On* album shot up the charts, proving that it was possible to make a socially conscious statement and still sell records. With its incredible arrangements by David Van De Pitte, *What's Going On* was, in my opinion, Marvin's greatest gift to the world of music. I'm sure it was way ahead of its time. It certainly wasn't typical of its time, due to its choice of material or its structure.

What's Going On was actually an album of firsts. It was Marvin's first self-written, self-produced album; the first concept album; and the first to have its lyrics printed on the jacket so that listeners could sing along. It was also said to be the first album on which an artist talked while singing through dubbing. (Dubbing was actually a technique called "stacking," which means to double the voices and/or instruments, and was pioneered in the early 1950s, when Les Paul and Mary Ford set the standard. Jo Stafford and Patti Page also had huge hits with the process early on, then along came Marvin doing all sorts of tricks with his voice in the studio.)

Even Berry Gordy had some good things to say about *What's Going On*. He called the album "a major smash," admitting that Marvin "came off just as sexy as when he sang his 'you' songs directly to women."

What's Going On produced three Top Ten singles: the title track, "Inner City Blues," and "Mercy Mercy Me." The enormous commercial success of the album had Marvin planning his return to live performances. He had not sung in public since the tragic death of Tammi Terrell.

He put performing on hold, however, to appear in the 1971 big-screen movie *Chrome and Hot Leather*. He had appeared in a television movie, a Danny Thomas–Aaron Spelling production called *The Ballad of Andy Crocker*, while I was overseas. The first TV movie to deal with the Vietnam War, it had a first-rate cast, including Lee Majors, Joey Heatherton, Bobby Hatfield, Agnes Moorhead, Pat Hingle, Peter Haskell, Jill Haworth, and Marvin, who got fourth billing. He didn't have much of a role, but the film was well received and he liked working on a Hollywood sound stage. Acting suited him; he wanted to do more.

However, unlike *The Ballad of Andy Crocker*, *Chrome and Hot Leather* didn't have much going for it. Along with Marvin, the cast included William Smith, Tony Young, Michael Haynes, and Peter Brown. Basically a motorcycle movie, the story was about the death of a girl murdered by a gang of bikers, and about her Green Beret fiance, who was out for revenge. The reviews were awful, ranging from "stupid" to "bomb." The best thing about the film, according to Marvin, was that it got acting out of his system and revived his interest in motorcycles. Marvin had always wanted a bike. Now, on his return from Hollywood, he got one. He also bought some undeveloped property in Washington state that he wanted to check out. The land purchase was hastily made, more as an excuse for the two of us to get away together, I suspected, than as a moneymaker for him.

Marvin and I had never roughed it in the woods as kids. My only experience with being out in the wilds was in Vietnam, and that was not a happy one. But we set out anyway, loaded to the hilt with the latest in camping equipment and gear. I'm sure he spent a small fortune on the tent, netting, cots, sleeping bags, pillows, cooking utensils, cook stove, butane, the works. If the Ritz-Carlton had a hotel nearby, it couldn't have been better equipped. Marvin charged everything, even though he didn't have a credit card. He was so well known now that all he had to do was give his manager's name and address.

Off we went in one of Marvin's flashy cars, with the camping equipment packed into the small trailer carrying his motorcycle hitched to the rear. I met Marvin in Detroit, and from there we headed west along Route 12 to Chicago, where we picked up Route 30, which took us westward through Illinois, Iowa, Nebraska, Wyoming, Idaho, into Oregon, and on up to the Washington border. We felt like a modern-day Lewis and Clark.

The scenery was sensational, with sprawling views of towering mountains and endless forests. Marvin's property was along the Cowlitz River, in the southern part of the state. It was impossible to tell its boundaries, since there were no markers anywhere, only rolling grasslands rising to distant elevations that reached into the clouds. Enough of the land was flat, which would have allowed Marvin to build, but I couldn't see him living in the wilderness. Neither could he, except for a night or two. We found a perfect spot to pitch our tent—or it would have been perfect, if we could have figured the thing out. So we planned on sleeping in the car, which was fine with both of us. We had everything we needed either with us or near us, even clear, fresh water from the nearby rushing river. The icy temperature of the water reminded us of our adventures as kids at the swimming hole in D.C. "Man, this is the life," Marvin sighed.

Once we got his motorcycle out of its trailer, we had a great time riding up and over the rolling hills, kind of like Steve McQueen in the final scenes of *The Great Escape*. Feeling the clear, fresh air against our faces was invigorating. It was so peaceful, except for the roar of the bike. We were loving our run through the wilds when suddenly we heard another sound, a deep, thunderous rumble that seemed to come from nowhere, and everywhere. Marvin slammed down on the brakes and we came to a sliding halt, almost throwing me off the back of the bike. "Did you hear that?" he stammered, his eyes wide as hubcaps.

"Why do you think my hair is standing up?" I replied.

"That's it," he said. "We're done here."

"I'm with you, Bro. Let's move!"

Marvin turned the bike around as the tires spun, sending us flying. We were almost halfway back to our campsite when we saw a big, black blob coming over the faraway hill. It wasn't Bigfoot, but it was huge, and coming our way, moving fast. At that point, Marvin screamed, "*It's a bear!*"

Being city kids, we'd never seen a live bear before, let alone one charging at us. So we did what we did 20-some years earlier when the neighborhood ruffians came charging. We ran—or, in this case, we *rode*—for our lives.

Once we got to the car we threw our stuff inside, rolled the bike into the trailer, and sped away in a flash. Marvin kept the motorcycle, but I don't know what happened to the property. I have a feeling he held on to it but lost it to the government when he had his money problems. At any rate, Marvin never mentioned wanting to rough it again.

It wasn't until Marvin's teenage years that he became a frustrated jock. Like singing, he initially thought sports would be a girl-magnet for him, so he tried his hand at football, basketball, golf, even boxing. He really wasn't very good at any of them. His feet were bad, which is why I always beat him when we raced. Outclassed as he was, he never packed it in. He always felt he had what it took to be an athlete.

As teenagers we had worked as caddies, thanks to our neighbor Mr. Hawkins, who got us jobs at Marbeck Country Club in D.C. As we grew older, we would drive around together, and whenever we'd see kids playing hoops, he'd stop the car and join them in their pickup games. Later, once Marvin had signed with Motown, he and Smokey Robinson became regulars on Detroit's Palmer Golf Course. Golf wasn't his game either, but he kept at it, betting on every round and always losing. One time, he had a big-time wager with Smokey that had Anna fuming, even during the early days of their marriage. Marvin had started out sailing across the course, barely blinking as he made putt after putt on the greens. He was so confident that he bet his house on Outer Drive on the next putt. It was only a short distance, and he could make it with ease, he thought. He missed. To rub it in, Smokey later drove Marvin and Anna past their former home and said, "Remember when you used to live there?"

The next thing I knew, Marvin announced that he was thinking of getting into professional football. "You're messing with me," I said on hearing that news.

"I'm serious, Bro," he replied. "I've been working out with Smokey, jogging, doing push-ups, jumping jacks, and all that to get into shape. Mel Farr and Lem Barney are getting me a tryout with the Lions."

"The Detroit Lions or Barnum and Bailey?"

"C'mon, don't even try to discourage me. Smokey said I'm insane but he's hanging in with me, because you know what?"

"What?"

"I'd rather catch a pass and score a touchdown in Tiger Stadium than rack up another gold record."

"I gotta see that," I said.

"You'll be the first to get tickets to the game," he told me.

True to his word, Marvin not only was invited to the Lions' training camp, he showed up on time. Marvin on time? "A first!" I exclaimed, teasing him.

He ignored my remark; I should have known why he wasn't in a playful mood. He didn't say it in so many words, but he admitted he didn't do very well. In other words, he got his butt kicked.

Marvin still wouldn't give up on sports, not yet anyway. He had another idea that had nothing to do with singing, he said.

"It's boxing, isn't it?" I asked.

"Why do you say that?"

"It's about the only thing you haven't tried, and you've always liked it." Growing up, Marvin and I were never allowed to hit anything. Since then he had overcome much of his shyness, and being rebellious and aggressive, I thought he might do fairly well in the ring. But then, his footwork was lousy.

"Maybe it's boxing and maybe it's not. I'm not saying what it is right now," he said stubbornly. "It might happen soon and it might happen later. I'll let you know."

I couldn't wait to hear. If it wasn't boxing, or even if it was, knowing Marvin, it had to be a stretch for him.

It's been said that Marvin had always wanted to play sports as a kid and Father wouldn't let him. Not true. When Marvin was young, the only thing on his mind was music. That's all he thought about, all he talked about. He loved his time with Father at the piano, and until he got into doo wop singing, his main outlet was church, where he played the organ and sang with the choir. Actually, we both sang in church because we loved it—and because it got us out of Bible study.

If Marvin had wanted to play sports in those days, he could have. His obligation to church took up only a portion of his time, and we certainly had lots of time to do kid things and get into trouble. Had Marvin been interested in sports in those days, things might have worked out differently for him as an adult.

Since Marvin's dabbling at acting in Hollywood, our adventurous trip to the Northwest, and his fling at sports, two years had passed since he had stepped on a stage. Although he had made news with *What's Going On,* he had been out of the limelight lately. The performer in him was hungering for attention. He knew that just the possibility of his resuming live performances would make headlines.

The first plan for Marvin's long-awaited return to the stage backfired badly. He had let it slip that he might perform at the inaugural Martin Luther King birthday commemoration in Atlanta. The excitement generated by a single uncredited report in *Soul Magazine* not only proved that Marvin's support was huge, it suggested it might even be greater than Reverend King's. Marvin abandoned all thoughts of making his live return at the event.

In the spring of 1972, Marvin was invited to attend a special celebration. Washington, D.C., had set aside May 1st as Marvin Gaye Day, and he was asked to perform. It was a huge honor for Marvin, but he was apprehensive and filled with indecision. And while he really didn't want to go, he felt he had to. It was Mother's persuading that made up his mind.

There was a motorcade, a morning tribute at his old high school, a VIP reception prior to a benefit concert at the Kennedy Center, a key to the city, and an official plaque signed by the mayor, all for Marvin. We all showed up, even Father, who saw his son perform professionally for the first time. Despite Marvin's nerves, he was polite, grateful, and enthusiastic as he received his tribute, then he was his suave, cool self as he sang onstage. Father said he was pleased with

Marvin's performance and the celebrations; he even told Marvin he was proud of him. Marvin beamed on hearing that, and knowing he finally had Father's support. Seeing Marvin and Father together, Mother got teary-eyed. I must admit I got a little choked up too. It had been way too long since I had felt a real bond between Father and his namesake, even though I couldn't help but wonder if that bond was more a tug of war.

By the end of the evening, after all the handshakes, smiles, and pats on the back, Marvin was saying he had stayed away way too long. Mother said she had never seen Marvin happier.

Marvin didn't stay long in D.C. He returned to Detroit, which had become a musical ghost town since Berry Gordy had moved his Motown operation to Los Angeles, during Marvin's "athletic" absence. "Where do I belong now?" Marvin asked. He certainly felt he no longer belonged in Detroit.

9

In January 1973, Marvin received an invitation from Stephen Hill, a Jamaican impresario who was setting up a benefit for the Boys Club of Trench Town, Kingston's poorest slum. Marvin didn't commit right away. The cause was good, but flying to Jamaica was another matter. Marvin had a hard time saying yes if flying was involved.

It wasn't until Hill mentioned that Bob Marley would also perform that Marvin agreed to go. He'd never met Bob Marley, but he felt linked to him through his music, which Marley used to bring about political change and to inspire his people.

Once Marvin stepped off the plane in Kingston, he was welcomed like royalty. Even though Jamaica was going through severe economic problems at the time, the people knew how to treat their guests; the island had long been a haven for the privileged, namely the European elite. During a guided tour following his arrival, Marvin was shown the polo clubs, shops, restaurants, tearooms, plantations, and stately homes once occupied by Noel Coward, Ian Fleming, and Errol Flynn. He saw the beautiful countryside: dense, green forests; limestone rock formations; ancient caves that contained underground rivers; and secluded beaches that pirates once used as hideaways. Then he was taken through the poor sections of the island, including

Trench Town. "I'm glad I'm here," Marvin said by phone, "and I sure hope I can do something to help the poor kids I've seen. There are more churches here than any other place in the world, but the schools are so far apart that many kids don't go—or can't go. It's sad to see these children just hanging out, wasting their days doing nothing."

The concert was held at Kingston's Carib Theater, before a full house that included Shirley Temple and her husband, Charles Black; all the proceeds went to the children's charity. Following the show, Jamaican Prime Minister Michael Manley presented Marvin with a key to the city and dedicated a section of private beach to him, a strip of land that would forever be Marvin's alone. (Reports that Marvin bought the property and planned to build a home there are not true.) His three-day visit to Jamaica led to Marvin's involvement in a charitable organization called "Save the Children."

Marvin returned to Detroit like a man without a care in the world, raving about the jerk chicken and Blue Mountain coffee, the island's famous "black gold." He couldn't sit still for long, though. "Changes are coming," he told me. "I feel like I belong in Detroit, and I do, but I'm being pulled away. It's not happening for me here. No way I'm going anywhere without taking you and the family with me. No way."

Ever since Marvin Gaye Day in D.C., Marvin felt a new closeness and harmony within the family, especially from the person whose acceptance he craved the most. He saw the smile on Father's face and felt the warmth of his hand when Father reached out to congratulate him. Family was so important to Marvin. It hurt him that he and Anna were continually at odds, or so it seemed, but they were still together. He mentioned that Anna and young Marvin also might feel like going with him whenever he left Detroit.

During the latter months of 1972, Marvin had traveled back and forth to Hollywood several times while he was working on the largely instrumental score for 20th Century Fox's slick crime-drama, *Trouble Man*. It was a new direction for Marvin. When the offer came, he grabbed it, inspired by the success of Isaac Hayes's score for *Shaft* the previous year. "The Theme from *Shaft*" had won the Academy Award for Best Song that year, and Marvin was hoping to duplicate that success with his theme for *Trouble Man*. It didn't happen, even though the title song, first released as a single, led to an album of songs from the film that sold really well. Filmed throughout Los Angeles, *Trouble Man* starred Robert Hooks, Paul Winfield, Ralph Waite, William Smithers, and Paula Kelly. It came and went without much fanfare. Marvin said, "I might have gotten a film score award if more people had seen the movie."

By the time Marvin decided to move to Los Angeles, he was fairly familiar with the sprawling city. Not familiar enough, however, to know exactly where to settle down. Besides, he was with Anna and little Marvin, who at eight years of age, wasn't so little anymore. As long as the relationship with Anna wasn't as solid as it once was, they thought it would be best to live for a time with Anna's sister, Gwen, in her Beverly Hills home on Benedict Canyon Drive.

Marvin was away from Benedict Canyon for days at a time, looking at apartments for himself as well as for studio space where he could work again. His frequent absences led to more arguments with Anna.

Within the next months Marvin found everything he was looking for, and more. He took a small apartment in Culver City. He designed and built his own recording studio on Sunset Boulevard in Hollywood, facilities he intended to rent out for income, and made a number of investments, which included ten thousand dollars to his friend Wally Amos, in exchange for a percentage of his Famous Amos Cookies company. He also started accumulating a fleet of fancy cars. Eventually he would have 14, two for each day of the week. Pretty good for someone who had never had a driver's license.

Most of Marvin's spending spree was handled through his newly formed Right On Productions. His biggest investment was the English Tudor–style home he bought for Mother and Father, on Gramercy Place, in the Crenshaw district of Los Angeles. The property was huge—it was actually two houses, the big house and the guest house next door—all of which was surrounded by a gated privacy wall.

The two-story main house had eight bedrooms, five bathrooms, a family room, living room, formal dining room, and an enormous kitchen where Mother would spend most of her time. The house next door looked much the same, only on a smaller scale. The lower floor was a garage; upstairs there was a spacious two-bedroom apartment.

When Marvin called from California to describe the property and tell us to get packed, Mother had a few words for him—that is, once she calmed down. "Marvin, I know you want to do all these wonderful things for us," she said, "and I know you're making good money, but be careful, honey."

"Don't worry, Mother, I'm doing good, real good."

"Listen to me, Marvin," she said. "You'll always be poor to somebody, and somebody will always be richer. Never be the poorest, never be the richest. Be happy with what you have."

"I'm happy, Mother," he told her. "I'll be even happier once you get out here and move into your new house."

Marvin had bought the house for Mother, as well as to bring the family to California—to have everyone close to him again. He got more than he bargained for. As time went on, the house always seemed to be full, not only with the immediate family, but with a continuing round of visiting relatives and friends.

It was at the house on Gramercy Place that Marvin first started thinking about his next album. He had a string of two consecutive gold albums to his credit, *What's Going On* and *Trouble Man*. He wanted another one. It wasn't until Marvin ran into Ed Townsend that the project came together.

Marvin had first met Ed, a songwriter and record producer, during his early days at Motown, and was immediately impressed. What first sold Marvin were Ed's credits: once Marvin discovered that Ed had worked with Nelson Riddle, that was it. After all, it was Riddle's great, driving arrangements that had only a few years earlier revived Frank Sinatra's recording career. Marvin, the Sinatra wannabe, had found his man.

Over ten years had passed since Marvin and Ed had seen each other. So much had happened in between that they actually had to be reintroduced by a mutual friend. The two got together, and before too long, they were collaborating on Marvin's next album. Marvin recalled, "When Ed told me he had a good idea for a song called 'Let's Get It On,' I knew immediately, or instinctively, that the phrase was a smash. Then he sat and played the melody for me and I was blown away. It was so beautiful. Then I just did the lyric and it worked.

"I hope it won't advocate promiscuity. I try to think that my records are honest, and that what I sing about should be dealt with honestly, not with promiscuity and muckiness, but I don't have any restrictions, no boundaries. I can't be dictated to or told what kind of music to release. I have to put out the kind of music my soul tells me to."

Most of the songs for the *Let's Get It On* album were recorded between March and June of 1973, at the Motown Hitsville studio, in Hollywood. Ed Townsend has long said that the original message in the words of the title were not about sex but "the business of getting on with life," and that is the feeling Marvin gave to the song when a demo version was first recorded on March 13th. That concept went out the window nine days later at the actual recording session when Ed walked in with a friend, Barbara Hunter, and her sixteen-year-old daughter, Janis.

A sophomore at Fairfax High School in Los Angeles, Janis had been infatuated with Marvin ever since her best girlfriend at the time told her to check out Marvin's *Trouble Man* album cover. Meeting Marvin thrilled Janis, and according to Marvin, she too was more than a thrill. Young and beautiful, with her slender figure, long black hair, perfect lips, light skin, and slim, freckled nose, she was a dream come true. "My heart was pounding at the sight of her," he said, "I had a song to cut, with her listening and looking at me. I don't know how I controlled myself and got through it. I thought I might have to sit down during the recording session or embarrass myself."

As Jan remembers, "He kept looking at me and I kept looking away because I was shy. At the same time, I tried to look back at him because I wanted him to think I was grown-up and sophisticated, and not just some young kid."

With the arrival of Jan, the final take of "Let's Get It On" took on a whole new meaning. Marvin later admitted that he had unknowingly abandoned the song's original concept to sing it straight from his heart. "I sang the way I felt," he said. "It was all spontaneous."

To that, Ed Townsend responded, "He could sing 'The Lord's Prayer' and it would have sexual overtones."

Once again, the songs Marvin sang reflected his mood. This time, unlike his past two albums, his mood was upbeat and sensual, even explicit at times. Marvin had fallen in love—or lust—which turned *Let's Get It On* into the most joyous personal statement, and into another gold album.

As Jan tried to let Marvin know at their first meeting, she definitely was not "just some young kid." Her father was jazz great Slim Gaillard, who had written and recorded several huge hits of the 1930s and 1940s, including "Cement Mixer (Put-ti, Put-ti)," "Flat Foot Floogie," and "Tutti Frutti." She was familiar with the music business, which made Marvin feel even closer to her. By the summer of 1973, they were living together.

Jan and Marvin found a house in a ruggedly remote section of Topanga Canyon, high in the nearby Santa Monica Mountains. The small house was far from fancy; it was much like the other rustic abodes that were scattered about the pine- and shrub-covered canyon hillsides. "This is horse country," Marvin said, "a bit of Bohemia. We love it up here. The views from our windows are incredible, and you hear sounds you never hear in the city. It's nature, man, it's music."

From the Topanga house, Marvin began to mastermind his full-blown return to performing. The publicity photos for *Let's Get It On* had him showing another new look. He had taken to wearing knitted skullcaps, and he wanted his fans to see him wearing them.

The skullcaps started when he received one as a gift. He liked the look, but they were more than a fashion statement to Marvin. He believed he was going bald on top, and he was, so the caps provided a cover-up. Once he had one, he wanted more. Wherever he went, especially on tour, his valet would check out the stores, and knowing what Marvin would be wearing onstage, would look for appropriate colors. His valet, Odell George, whom Marvin called "Gorgeous George," would often decorate the caps with silver studs, threads, or other detailing.

Marvin also put together a new team, made up of people he felt he could trust completely. He asked me to work with him as a kind of jack-of-all-trades, so to speak. I was looking forward to going on the road with him, until the schedule got off to a rough start. We had to cancel one show that was to take place in San Francisco during November 1973. Marvin blamed the cancellation on personal problems, which he was able to resolve in time for the rescheduled concert, this time across the bay, in Oakland.

The night of January 4th was memorable for several reasons. It was Marvin's first real concert in four years, and it was to be the source for his hit album *Marvin Gaye Live!* That evening also marked the debut of a trick that Marvin and I played on audiences time and again.

Since we had always looked alike, I used to tease Marvin about working hard to keep us looking that way. When I grew a beard following my stint in Vietnam, he said, "Cut that thing off, man. It makes you look old." I didn't, so he grew one too.

Because we also sounded so much alike when we talked and sang, Marvin thought it would be great fun to fool audiences by having me go out instead of him and do the concert. "No way," I told him. He wouldn't give up; he had to put one over on the crowds during his performances.

Part of my working with Marvin was to open his concerts by introducing him. So when the lights dimmed that first evening in Oakland, the crowd began to roar as I walked out onstage, thinking I was the star. I had prepared and rehearsed an introduction, but all that went out the window with the uproar. My mind went blank, and there I was, nervous and alone facing all those shouting, screaming fans. Then they began chanting "MARVIN ... MARVIN ... MARVIN ..." but I wasn't Marvin! It took a few minutes before the noise quieted down a bit, but once it did the crowd anxiously waited for Marvin—er, me—to say something. I don't know where it came from but all I could think to say was, "Ladies and gentlemen, here is my brother and yours." Raising my arm, I pointed offstage to where Marvin was waiting to come on, then looked out at the audience. I saw nothing but blank faces, staring in disbelief. I motioned for Marvin to come out, but he wouldn't move. He was behind the curtain, doubled up, laughing at me. I didn't know what to do next, so I ran offstage as Marvin, still laughing, sauntered out. The roar started all over again. The same thing happened every time we pulled that trick, only from then on I knew what to expect.

At a jazz festival in San Diego, we did the red suit–white suit routine. We had identical suits made, only they were in different colors. Wearing the red suit, I walked out onstage first, and the crowd went crazy thinking I was Marvin. Instead of stopping, I kept walking until I exited the other side of the stage. The second I disappeared Marvin came out on the opposite side wearing his white suit. There was a sudden hush as everyone looked on in disbelief, wondering how Marvin had changed suits and made it to the opposite side so quickly. I was then brought out again, and the gag became pretty obvious, except everyone had to know who I was.

Once again, Marvin had a new look for his fans. This time he wore denim, reflecting his new country lifestyle, only he jazzed it up with sparkles on his collars and cuffs—and feet. Marvin had discovered Fred Slatten, a Hollywood shoe designer who had made a name for himself designing flamboyant platforms for the likes of Sonny and Cher, Elton John, Gene Simmons, Nancy Sinatra, and as Slatten put it, "Every *Playboy* centerfold for 15 years."

For his debut of Slatten's platform footwear, Marvin wanted high-topped silver platforms, covered from top to bottom with glittering silver and strung up with shocking red laces. And that's what he got.

As usual, Marvin was always petrified before facing audiences. Now he had more to worry about, thinking that maybe the gags would fall flat, or his new look, or even the entire concert. There was no questioning the atmosphere backstage. It was always bedlam.

A perfectionist, Marvin coached me on the various concert details, which had to come off perfectly or he'd get really upset. Another part of my job was to check him before he went onstage to see that he looked good. That was important! He always had to look good for the ladies. One night, however, during a last-second rush, I overlooked something: his fly was unzipped. In front of a sold-out arena of his fans and a national TV audience, he started singing, then bending, twisting, and dipping, and there were moments when his pants would separate in front. The ladies went nuts. They couldn't see anything, but the first few rows were sure leaning forward.

Marvin was halfway through his number when he saw me motioning to him to zip up. Trying to look cool, he turned around and quickly closed his fly without missing a beat. He was embarrassed to have such a thing happen onstage and before the cameras, but not that embarrassed. The number went over so big that he had thoughts of working it into his act. The demand for front-row seats soared after that.

It is definitely not true, as one of Marvin's biographers claimed, that he masturbated before his performances. How could anyone make up such a thing? Marvin had no ritual before he went onstage. Even if he did, masturbating would not have been it. Doing that may relieve a certain tension, but not the tension you have before performing. It saps your energy, and he needed all the energy and sexual drive he could muster before going onstage.

Most performers will tell you that the feeling you get before performing is the worst feeling in the world. Talking is difficult enough when you're nervous, but try singing. How do you get that smooth, confident sound when you're shaking inside? You can't breathe, but you *have* to breathe.

It takes extraordinary strength to put on a good face night after night and perform up to expectations. Marvin's stage fright was always so great. It was not only a fear of walking out onstage, but of not being able to please his audiences. He once admitted to an interviewer, "Am I comfortable onstage? I nearly die out there. No, I'm never comfortable onstage. I'm full of butterflies. I don't know how I manage to get through any performances, ever. I'm an artist. It's not my nature to be an exhibitionist. I'm kind of an 'in' person. I'm quiet and I like to be by myself. Rather reclusive. It's difficult for me to perform, but once I'm out there and I can feel the love and energy that's coming back to me, it's difficult to get me *off* the stage."

Marvin never wanted to disappoint anyone who had come to see him. For years, he had said "no" to backstage visitors who offered to make him "feel better" before his performances, but there were also times, no matter where he was, that he would be caught at a low point. In the beginning, once he finally gave in, he thought, "What's the harm? It's just this one time." But saying no became harder and harder for Marvin, especially when he felt so good going out onstage. In time, "What's the harm?" became "Why not?" Those are words I will never forget. They became his standard reply whenever I tried to reason with him. Nothing seemed to matter, not even the mention of Jan, who was waiting for him at home—or the child that he only recently learned was on its way.

It was almost as impossible to get Marvin to mind the clock, which was a job in itself. Marvin was always late, late on purpose, even if the minutes were ticking away till showtime; his lateness was another sign of his rebellious character. Marvin liked living on the edge, mainly at airports where we always had to keep our fingers crossed. He hated to wait at boarding gates as much as he hated to fly, so he dawdled through airport walkways acting every bit the star, hoping people would recognize him and want his autograph. Everyone was "Baby," no matter who they were or what their age. It seemed I was forever telling him, "Hurry up, Marvin, let's go!"

We were on the road when an incident occurred that began to cloud Marvin's thinking. One of his lady fans had become totally infatuated with him, which had Marvin feeling flattered, until he learned that the lady's husband was out to kill him. After that, Marvin was put under guard until the man was apprehended. Years later, there would be talk of a similar incident, only there would be no angry husband. But a seed of fear had been planted in Marvin's mind.

10

"No more bad news," Marvin said. "Don't tell me no more. I don't want to hear it." Like it or not, bad news always seemed to reach him.

In September 1974, Marvin received a phone call asking him to take part in a planned memorial concert for Quincy Jones. "A memorial concert?" Marvin asked, his voice sinking with each word. According to the latest reports, Quincy Jones was near death. He had undergone a delicate operation for a severe brain aneurysm, and the outlook wasn't good. If he lived, he would either be brain-damaged, blind, or paralyzed. "He's not going to make it," the caller dimly told Marvin. "We're getting everyone together to pay tribute to him."

It was the fastest I'd ever heard Marvin say, "I'll be there." Then he broke down.

When the caller said they were getting everyone together, that wasn't far from the truth. "Everyone" included just about every single person Quincy had ever worked with or known, and that included the biggest names in show business. "All his friends were there for him," Marvin reported on his return. "Even Quincy was there."

"What?" I said. "I thought he was ..."

"We all did, and that's what made it so special. Just having him with us, sitting off to the side, was a huge thrill, and gave us all hope."

Still, the doctors said there was little chance that Quincy would make it. He was fighting for his life, still facing a series of risky operations. If he survived those, ahead was a long period of recuperation. Knowing all that, his doctors allowed him to attend his own memorial—kind of like Tom Sawyer, only better, because it wasn't fiction. Of course, Quincy did survive to continue his career as one of the greatest, and most-awarded, composers and producers of all time.

As Quincy battled to live, Jan was in the hospital giving birth to Nona Aisha Gaye, nicknamed "Pie." Marvin was so proud of his beautiful little daughter. He couldn't stop hugging her and kissing her. He wanted nothing more than to hold her in his arms.

Fourteen months later, Jan was back in the hospital giving birth to my namesake, Frankie Christian Gaye. When Frankie—or "Bubby," as he was called—was born, I'd never seen Marvin more proud. What made little Frankie's arrival so special was that he was scheduled to be born on my birthday, November 15th.

There were lots of bets going on in the hospital as to the exact time the baby would make his arrival. Marvin was in and out of Jan's room, encouraging her to make it happen, then pacing the halls (which thrilled the nurses), before returning to prompt an extra push and grunt. As it neared midnight we were all sweating it out; poor Jan was exhausted, and the baby had yet to arrive. Then midnight passed and the pressure was off everyone except Jan. Little Frankie missed my birthday by only ten minutes, but that was fine. He was finally here, healthy, and happy. As the nurses gathered around him, one of them cooed, "Isn't he cute?"

Turning, Marvin gave her a gentle jab and said, "What about me?"

While Marvin and Jan were building a family, his world was falling apart around him. He was in trouble with Anna, who was still legally his wife; with the Internal Revenue Service; and with Motown. Too often, however, he acted as if his problems were nothing, even as they began to smother him. He believed he was indestructible, that money was out there for the taking. Just reach out and grab it. The fact is, too many of the people surrounding him kept building him up as a "star," feeding his ego and draining him dry.

I tried to keep his feet on the ground, which wasn't easy. There were times when I found myself sounding a lot like Father, preaching to him. I told him, "Let these people exalt you, but don't believe them. You're still Marvin Gaye my big brother, and you'll always be that. They're exalting Marvin Gaye the singer, and that's only a surface exaltation. It's fleeting. The minute you stop singing they'll move on to someone else." I had the feeling he listened to me as carefully as he had listened to Father.

Marvin's marriage to Anna came to a legal end in March 1977, and with that he owed her $600,000 in alimony. There was no way he could come up with the money, so his attorney, Curtis Shaw, arranged with Motown that she receive the advance, plus all the earnings, from his next Motown album, which he was obligated to deliver according to his contract. That was fine with Marvin. He said he'd already written off the album anyway. That may have been what he had planned to do, but when it came to creating the songs for the album, he poured himself into it—plus a lot of Anna—and the result was one of his most personal creations to date. Facetiously titled *Here, My Dear,* the album basically chronicled Marvin's married life with Anna, through such songs as "Loving You," "When Did You Stop Loving Me, When Did I Stop Loving You?", "Anger," "You Can Leave but It's Going to Cost You," and "Falling in Love Again." Released in 1978, the album was a rare commercial flop for Marvin, earning less than half of what he owed Anna, which had him pleased with himself. Even if it had been a hit, he wouldn't have made any money from it.

To make matters worse, the IRS was after him for unpaid back taxes. He also faced lawsuits by an ex-manager, a former business manager, and various collection agencies for unpaid bills, among them a sizable $14,000 he had run up at the Chateau Marmont, Hollywood's famed hideaway hotel on the Sunset Strip. "He stiffed us for thousands in unpaid room rent," says Raymond Sarlot, co-owner of the hotel at the time. "We billed him but nothing happened. Later, we submitted a bill to his estate but discovered there was nothing there. After that, what were we to do? Say we sued Marvin Gaye?"

On top of everything else, his relationship with the press was souring. No one could get to him during the morning hours. Since he usually slept till noon, all interviews were arranged for after lunchtime, and even then, seeing him or getting him to talk was a gamble. It wasn't unlike him to disappear in the middle of an interview.

As the pressures kept mounting so did his drug use. It had once been only an occasional thing, just to help him overcome his stage fright. Now it had become alarmingly frequent. Even though Marvin never carried any money with him—no cash, no credit cards—he still found ways to spend huge gobs of money, mainly on frivolous and foolish expenditures. Until word of his situation got around, the name Marvin Gaye carried a lot of clout.

In the late summer of 1977, desperately in need of money, Marvin turned to the only means he knew of raising cash: a national tour. The money came in, and the money went out. People who knew Marvin well regarded him as an artist, not a businessman.

Since moving to California, Marvin's life was filled with more turmoil than ever. He had started a new family with Jan; toured extensively (performing in some cities, postponing and canceling in others); and moved from Topanga Canyon to a high-rise apartment in Brentwood, then to a Spanish-style ranch estate in the Hidden Valley section of the San Fernando Valley, outside Los Angeles. He faced numerous lawsuits and a lingering divorce action, he made money, he lost money, and he saw his relationship with Jan start to crack. "It's all my fault," he told me. "I've done crazy things I shouldn't be doing. I love Jan with all my heart, and I love being with her. I can be a dog sometimes, and I know it, but we'll work it out."

Marvin didn't say it in so many words, but I knew he had cheated on Jan. He didn't have to go on the road to do it, either. There were corners in Hollywood where he could find action any hour of the day or night.

Jan knew how to upset Marvin, too. She wanted to sing and he wouldn't let her. He admitted she had a good voice, good enough to be a star on her own, but he never gave in. I knew the feeling.

Surprisingly, Marvin did ask Janis and me to sing with him, as background singers on his recording of "Got to Give It Up," which became the entire side four of his two-LP *Live at the London Palladium* album. The actual concert, recorded overseas in September 1976, had filled only three sides. Needing to fill the fourth, Marvin uncharacteristically caved in to Motown's demands that he write and record disco, the big musical craze that swept the country during the mid-'70s. He had repeatedly rejected the label's cries, but with a full side available, he did disco *his* way, by putting together a nearly 12-minute-long dance-party song, which wound up No. 1 on the charts, despite starting out basically as an impromptu studio-recorded jam session.

The success of "Got to Give It Up" brought Marvin more money to spend, which he did at his usual wrong places, and for his usual wrong reasons. Throughout his lifetime, Marvin had always ignored problems when he was faced with them. He simply went his own way, doing his own things, his way. No matter what, he could not change the way he lived.

Marvin's life couldn't have been more complicated than it was at this time, and for one of the few times in his life, his problems had become almost impossible to ignore. There were more lawsuits—four of his musicians were suing him for back pay—and Jan had threatened to leave him if they didn't get married. With all the uncertainties, marriage was the last thing on his mind. But he still loved Jan, and he worshipped his children.

On October 10th, 1977, Jan and Marvin were married in New Orleans, with little Nona and Frankie at their sides. Marvin sent photos of the wedding home, and everyone looked great. Jan, his young bride, had lilies of the valley in her long hair, which framed her face. She looked especially beautiful in her white gown with long sleeves. Marvin wore a white suit with a red tie and handkerchief.

The wedding took place during a break in Marvin's national tour, which had begun only weeks earlier as a desperate quick fix to his money problems. Again, Marvin wanted a new look for his show. He got that by adding more dancers, and even considered doing a few steps himself. Since he was such a dud at dancing, he knew he had to sharpen what little skill he had, particularly for one of his numbers, "Hitch Hike," a crowd favorite. He hired Paul Lawrence Kennedy, a Los Angeles–based pop dance choreographer and teacher who had also worked with Gladys Knight and the Pips, the Temptations, and Michael Jackson. Kennedy not only choreographed Marvin's "Hitch Hike" number, but selected songs from his *Here, My Dear* album.

The money from the national tour came and went in typical Marvin fashion. Although he had earlier sworn he would never again record for Motown, he soon found himself in contract negotiations with the label. He held out for as long as he could, mainly because he didn't trust Berry Gordy. But when he was offered a seven-year contract, he signed. It wasn't the long term that swayed him; he simply couldn't resist the promised money for his initial two albums—money that was beyond his expectations—as well as the increased advances that were supposed to come down the line.

As the IRS tightened its grip on Marvin, he filed for bankruptcy. Even with the advance money he was to receive from Motown, he knew he'd never be able to pay off the government. Motown couldn't help him there the way it had in negotiating his divorce settlement with Anna. After all, he reasoned, it was the Motown accountants who had gotten him into trouble with the government to start with. Marvin's debt was so huge, and while he never really knew the actual amount of the debt, he estimated it could have been as high as six million dollars, which meant he stood to lose everything. His homes, his cars, his investments, his recording studio. They couldn't take away his earning power, however, or the crowds who came to see and hear him.

In early 1979, as *Billboard* magazine ranked Marvin among its Top Ten pop performers of all time, he began doing guest shots on TV and planning yet another tour. In between, he'd spend time with Jan and the kids. But married life was becoming as shaky as his hold on the house. He told me that he had been happier with Jan before they were married. "Now that we've made it legal, I feel trapped," he said. It wasn't the vows or a piece of paper that made a difference. Marvin had learned that Jan was seeing Rick James, an up-and-coming Motown star. Then Jan was gone. She had taken the kids and moved in with her mother, in Hermosa Beach.

Marvin left town to finish his tour. He had a few concert dates in the Southwest, he said, and on his return, the two of us were going to Las Vegas. "Fine," I said. "When do you open?"

"There's no show. We're going to see my guy, Andy Price. He's fighting Sugar Ray Leonard at Caesar's Palace." Sugar Ray was the welterweight champ, and Caesar's was the prime Vegas venue. The fight was being played up in the press. "It'll be on national TV," said Marvin, "but I've got to be there. If Andy wins I could get a fat paycheck."

"Nice," I replied, trying to sound encouraging. "Hope that happens."

I didn't know much about Andy Price other than what I'd read recently in the papers, so it came as a surprise when Marvin told me that he had been backing Price since early 1978. The fighter's nickname was "Hawk," and in the year and a half he had been with Marvin, he had gone undefeated in six fights. Surprisingly, the papers were giving the relative newcomer a chance against Sugar Ray. I wanted him to win for Marvin's sake, but I couldn't help feeling that Marvin was foolish to invest his money on an unknown.

"One other thing," Marvin said. "Mother's coming with us."

"Mother?" I repeated. "Why?"

"I want to show her a good time," he said. "She deserves it."

"Okay," I replied, not quite sure that was the real reason for asking her to come along. Could he have wanted a shoulder to cry on if his fighter failed him?

We left Los Angeles—Marvin, Mother, and I—on September 27th, during a heat wave, only to find the temperature climbing even higher as we traveled the long, desolate highway through the desert. Mother was all eyes, so excited about her first visit to Las Vegas. Seeing all the fancy hotels and bright lights, even the names of the stars who were appearing in the showrooms, didn't impress her as much as the casinos. She fell in love with the slot machines at first sight, and she couldn't wait to crank a few handles. "No thinking, just pull," she said happily. "Sit and have fun, and maybe get lucky. It makes my worries go away."

Mother swore she would not drop more than two dollars in nickels into the machines. That was her limit. No more than that. Never. And what happened? She hit the jackpot! "What's wrong?" she cried, when the machine began making a racket with its bells and buzzers. "What did I do? Did I break something?" She apologized until she was told what had really happened. Then her eyes got watery. "I'm rich!" she shrieked. "Just let me live to spend it."

I pleaded with her to put the money away and leave while she was a winner, but she'd have none of that.

"I came here with two dollars in my hand. I now have over 50. Leave me alone."

Mother kept playing and playing. She didn't lose all of the 50 dollars; she had set aside two dollars in quarters, and she walked away with more than that. She was true to her word.

That night the three of us saw Diana Ross's show at Caesar's Palace. Her solo career was on a new high. Since leaving the Supremes, she had starred in three major movies, received an Academy Award nomination, become Motown's pop diva, and now she was headlining in Las Vegas's top showroom.

Marvin and Diana had gone through a few rough times together. In 1973, for instance, Motown had paired them for an album of duets, an album that Marvin had definitely not wanted to make. He'd promised himself "no more duets" after Tammi Terrell's death, but there he was in the studio with Diana. True to form, Marvin had wandered in late, and to make matters worse, he was smoking a joint. "Diana was pregnant and the smoke bothered her," he told me. "She got all uppity, and so did I. It was all my fault." Unable to work together, they recorded their parts separately.

In the years since the ill-fated recording session, Marvin and Diana had become soul mates again, forever linked by their Motown association—their successes and trials with the label. Now Marvin was anxious to see Diana again. He had hoped to sneak us to our table at Caesar's without being noticed, but that was impossible. As Mother, Marvin, and I walked along the aisle, the showroom crowd began to buzz, then suddenly everyone was standing, cheering, and applauding. Marvin's shy grin spread from ear to ear as he waved back. Mother was beaming.

Part of Diana's show was to walk around to the tables and hand the mike to people to sing. When she got to our table, she handed the mike to Marvin, and her show suddenly turned into a Marvin Gaye concert. "Gimme that thing!" Diana said, grabbing back the mike. Marvin laughed, Diana laughed, and the crowd went crazy. After the show we all went back to Diana's dressing room for a hug-fest. Berry Gordy was there. Marvin sat down with him and the two of them actually had a nice, peaceful conversation. It wasn't the first time, I know, but seeing them together like that was rare anymore.

Marvin was still on an emotional high the next night, believing his fighter would win. "We can do it, we can do it," he kept mumbling. "We have to do it!" A win, Marvin was certain, would turn his life around and end his financial mess. It was worth millions to him down the line, he said.

The fight ended with less than three minutes to go in the first round. Andy "Hawk" Price had become Sugar Ray's punching bag. He made it look easy. Marvin was sick.

The ride back to Los Angeles was a long one. It didn't help that Mother and I were with Marvin. He had nothing to say; he simply kept to himself as he wallowed in his dark thoughts.

If Marvin was hoping for positive news once we got home, he didn't get it. In fact, the news he received a short time later was far worse than he could have imagined. Jan was nowhere to be found. She had gone off somewhere with Teddy Pendergrass.

Marvin and Teddy had been friends for several years, since 1977, when the former lead singer for Harold Melvin and the Blue Notes opened for Marvin on road dates. They clicked from the start, and it wasn't long before Teddy was hanging out with Marvin and Jan backstage in Marvin's dressing room. During shows, Teddy would stand in the wings—watching Marvin perform, gaining pointers on how to hold an audience, how to move his body, phrase a lyric, punch a word to emphasize its romantic or sexual intent. Marvin was flattered to learn that he had been Teddy's inspiration ever since Teddy had been a teenager. To give the young singer more recognition, Marvin would bring him back onstage during his own show, encouraging the crowd to give the "rising new star" a big hand. It wasn't unusual for Marvin, Jan, Teddy, and his date to get together after a performance for a late evening on the town.

Like Marvin, Teddy was tall, lean, handsome, and smooth. Though they had different styles (Teddy's voice was stronger, for one thing), they both wore beards and projected a sexy image. It came as no surprise to Marvin when Teddy's career took off strong. His albums didn't go gold, they went platinum. Marvin was happy for Teddy; he never considered him a threat as a singer. He never thought of him as a threat to his marriage, either, what was left of it, that is.

Marvin felt betrayed. He was in an ugly mood when he called to say he was taking off again. This time he was not just leaving town, he was leaving the country.

11

Marvin scared me. Hearing he was leaving the country, without any other explanation, had me thinking he was going to disappear again, sneaking off to dwell on his problems. It was bad enough when he hid behind closed doors in the house, rarely to show himself for days at a time. At least I knew where he was when he did that. Now I didn't know what to think. Marvin wasn't always a man of many words. There were times when you wanted him to talk, and he wouldn't. Then, again, there were times when you couldn't keep him quiet.

It wasn't until the next day that Marvin had more to say about his future plans. He was going on tour again, this time to Hawaii for concerts in November, then to Japan for three weeks of performances in Tokyo, Nagasaki, and Osaka. "Have your passports ready," he said. "You and Mother are coming with me." He sounded upbeat, eager to leave.

Mother wasn't sure about the long trip or the time away from home. "Do they have slot machines in those places?" she asked.

"I'm not sure," I answered. "Maybe in Japan." Just the possibility had her packing. Besides, she knew we'd be home within a month, which really wasn't that long. Marvin had to be back in California to perform at a big New Year's Eve celebration in Long Beach.

On the day of our departure, Marvin seemed unusually uptight. He kept pushing Mother and me to "hurry it up" so we wouldn't miss the plane. We had plenty of time, but he wanted to "Go, go, go!" As we left for the airport, he turned to look back at the house, as if for the last time. "Did you forget something?" Mother asked.

"Just checking to see everything's all right," he replied softly. "I love that place."

I saw the curtains in Father's upstairs bedroom window part for a second, then close.

At the airport, Marvin wasn't his dawdly self. He kept pushing us forward, eager to get on the plane. Only after we were in the air and on our way, did he seem to relax. He stayed that way until we boarded a plane again in Japan for our return flight home. He kept looking out the window and acting jittery; he refused food when it came time to eat. It wasn't until the plane was about to land in Hawaii for refueling that he turned to me and said, "This is where I get off, Frankie. I can't go the rest of the way."

His words startled me. "What's wrong?" I asked. "Where are you going?"

"I don't know right now, but I can't go home. I'm scared."

"Scared of what?"

"They'll grab me or something. They're after me and all I got."

"But your show. What about Long Beach?"

Marvin laughed. "That's the least of my troubles. I've got nothing to go back to. My homes, my studio ... they're grabbing almost everything. I can't handle being there. I'm better off away from it all."

Mother cried as Marvin departed the plane in Hawaii, even as the two of us returned to Los Angeles without him.

"We'll see him again soon," I said, as if saying a few hopeful words would make us both feel better. Inside, I wondered if I'd ever see him again.

Back in Los Angeles, we got word from Marvin that he had settled on the island of Maui, and he was living in an old van he'd parked
on a bluff overlooking the beach. "It's a great life," he said. "Sorta like
I'm on vacation. Except for some sprinkles every day, the weather's
good. Warm, just like the water."

"And nobody bothers you?"

"I wouldn't say that. Word's gotten out that I'm here. People keep
coming around to bring me whatever. A lot of partying going on,
you know what I mean?"

I did know what he meant, and I didn't like it. "How long you
going to keep this up, Marvin?" I asked.

"No telling, man. I just want to lose myself for a while."

"What about the European tour? Isn't that coming up pretty
soon?"

"That's off for now. I don't need any more of that, too much pressure. All I want is to clear my head and try to get back into shape."

I heard voices in the background. "Where are you?" I asked.
"Where are you calling from?"

"The hotel," he answered. "There's a big, fancy resort near where
I'm hanging out. They know me here. Bubby's with me."

"Bubby? How did he get there?"

"It's a long story, Bro."

"Is Jan there?"

"I called her to try and patch things up. She told me she wasn't
with Teddy anymore, and she still loved me. I told her I still loved
her, too, and wanted her to be with me. She came with the kids,
both of them, and it was good for a while, but I couldn't get over
her being with Teddy. We did some screaming, I even started to get
violent with her. It was bad, real bad. She took off after that."

"She left the kids with you?"

"No."

"But you said..."

"She took Nona and Bubby with her. I got Bubby back later."

"How did that happen?"

"Let's just say a little someone in the family was here, Frankie, and let it go."

"C'mon, Marvin."

"Let it go," he said again.

"You'll tell me later?"

"We'll see," he said. "Maybe later."

The only "little someone" in the family who would do absolutely anything for Marvin was our little sister, Sweetsie. She'd follow him about, actually cling to him when he came home for a visit. She had to be close to him, feel like she was part of the excitement. When Marvin traveled to London for concerts and the taping of *Live at the London Palladium* in 1976, Sweetsie was there. If Marvin wanted something, good or bad, all he had to do was ask. I had the feeling Sweetsie was somehow involved in getting Bubby away from Jan and out to Hawaii with Marvin. She was, but it wasn't the way I had figured. Marvin never did tell me how she did it; Sweetsie told me, much later on, long after it happened.

It seems that one Friday night while Marvin was living his beachcomber life on Maui, Sweetsie received a phone call from Jan, who needed a babysitter for the evening. According to Sweetsie, she told Jan to bring little Bubby over to the house. It wasn't much later that Jan dropped Bubby off, then left without mentioning anything about the child being sick.

Mother was worried about Bubby from the start. But when Jan didn't return that evening or the next day, she had Sweetsie on the phone trying to track her down. When that failed, Mother told Sweetsie to call Marvin in Hawaii. "Bring him to me," Marvin said, and Sweetsie did.

On Monday, Jan called to say she was coming to get Bubby. Instead of hearing "Come and get him," she got the news that Bubby was with Marvin. "Jan was so furious," Sweetsie reported, "that she and her mother threatened to press kidnapping charges against me."

Now Mother had more to worry about than Marvin and her young grandson. If Marvin was in no condition to honor his European tour dates, how could he care for Bubby? And who were all those people who kept coming to see him? Mother certainly wasn't happy seeing Bubby go off to Hawaii, but things were happening way too fast.

Less than a week later Mother received a call from Marvin.

He needed help, he said, not only with Bubby, but with money. "Those diamonds I gave you are worth a lot. Bring them with you, please. You're my only hope." Before he hung up, he told her, "Pray for me, Mother, because I think I'm going to die." He mentioned wanting to go on to another life.

Mother left that afternoon carrying her diamonds and a batch of Marvin's favorite fried chicken. She arrived on Maui in the mid-afternoon, Hawaii time, only to find Marvin sleeping in the shade of his van, looking all scraggly, like a lost soul. Bubby was playing all by himself, close to the edge of the bluff. "I yelled Marvin's name real loud," she told me later, "as I grabbed the child into my arms. Marvin opened his eyes real slow and looked up at me. 'How long has *this* been going on?' I wanted to know. He just kept looking at me ... and started to cry."

Mother reported that she got Marvin and Bubby cleaned up, then they drove to a pawnbroker on the island. The diamonds were worth much more than Marvin received, about twice as much, she claimed, but that was still enough to pay a few months' rent on a condo in Lahaina, a historic whaling port turned tourist mecca on the southeast tip of Maui. With Mother's help, Marvin slowly began to become human again. They took long walks around Wharf Street and the village, with little Bubby tagging along, as they visited souvenir shops and saw the local high spots, like the old Court House; the tall ship *Carthaginian*, permanently moored in the harbor; and the Pioneer Inn, with its famous barroom, where Ernest Hemingway was said to have hung out. They even rented a jeep for a day trip across the island to drive up the slope of Haleakala, Maui's towering volcano. The biggest disappointment, Marvin told me, was the road to Hana. "Everyone said, 'You've got to take that drive. It's so beautiful.' Well, let me tell you, we drove up and up this narrow, winding, curvy road for hours and hours, past little signs pointing to this and that, which you can't see from the road, going slower and slower because you get in back of all these pokey cars and you can't pass them because the road's too narrow and twisty, and you think, 'Will we ever get to this place?' Then you get to Hana and what's there but a bunch of lazy old dogs lying on the road and a run-down old shack of a store that sells overpriced soft drinks and postcards. You wish you were back down on flat land, but you have to go through it all again, all the winding, twisting, slow-motion driving, only this time downhill. The greenery is nice, but you definitely want to be out of there *fast*. It's agonizing. Never, never, *never* again! Oh, and stay off the liquids if you ever come this way. There's no place to stop. Did I say 'agonizing'?!"

Mother remained with Marvin and Bubby for nearly two months. She was glad she was able to go, but she wished they would have returned with her. She begged Marvin, but he said no. She worried that he would slip back into his old way of living. She had every reason to worry.

"I'm trying to keep myself together," he said during a phone call several weeks after Mother's departure, "but I feel myself falling back again. There's been nothing but bad news from Los Angeles and the law. It's getting me all down."

From the sound of his voice I could tell he was really dragging and drugging. "Too much doing nothing, Marvin," I told him. "You need to get busy."

"What I need is money, man. I need an infusion of cash."

"I'd help if I could, you know that. But there's got to be some-body out of all the ..."

"I think of all the people who've held their hands out to me," he interrupted, "and I never let them down. Now I hold mine out and nothing happens."

"What about Little Stevie, Wally Amos, Frankie Beverly, Smokey?"

"Frankie Beverly? I heard stories about him and Jan. What a surprise, huh? And the others, well ..."

"Even Smokey?"

"Smokey was here, working a concert date in Honolulu and he came over to see me."

"He should be good for ..."

"Nothin'," Marvin said, quickly cutting me off.

According to Smokey, when he arrived at Marvin's place he found the door open and guys sleeping on the floor. Marvin was high on coke, even admitted to having a "toot" problem, but said he could stop whenever he wanted.

Marvin told Smokey he had a new plan. His European concerts were back on, he said, but he needed a chance to regroup, to clear his head so he could start writing again. More than anything, he told Smokey, he needed cash because his lawyers were draining him. He asked Smokey if he could spare five thousand dollars.

As Smokey remembers, he told Marvin he didn't have that kind of cash on him, and that he would have to think about it.

Smokey's response angered Marvin, and he lashed back. "Think about what? In the old days you wouldn't have thought a second about loaning a friend five G's."

Smokey said he still had to think about it, and that he'd call Marvin when he got back to Los Angeles.

Marvin was deeply hurt. Smokey had always come through for him; they were best friends. Marvin was certain Smokey wouldn't let him down. There still was a chance he would say yes.

Marvin waited for Smokey to get back to the mainland, then called him from Maui. He'd had time to think over Marvin's request; his reply was negative. He knew how Marvin would spend the money, and it wasn't for food or to pay his rent.

Marvin turned on Smokey, then hung up. He wouldn't speak to him again for nearly three years.

When Marvin told me what had happened, I stuck up for Smokey. "You can't blame him, Marvin. Think about it. He did the right thing. He knew he'd only be throwing his money away." Tough love.

As the press began to speculate that Marvin's career was over, he was battling with himself. The craving for stardom and the spotlight that had spurred him on since childhood was still there, and while he was never a fighter in the physical sense, he could fight with determination—if only he could get his mind together. His growing reputation as "the Judy Garland of the soul world" hit a nerve. "I can get involved again, and I want to," he told me. "All I have to do is figure out where I want to go."

He wanted to write again, but to write again he needed money. It helped when his old friend Harvey Fuqua came through for him. It helped too when Curtis Shaw, his attorney, told him the bankruptcy court had given Motown an order to advance him funds, even though he was a debtor, because recording was his primary means of earning money.

Marvin started writing again for an album he called *Love Man*. With Bubby in tow, he island-hopped from Maui to Oahu, where he rented a two-bedroom apartment, called his musicians, and began recording. More good news came when Jeffrey Kruger called—he was the British promoter who earlier had set up the European tour that had been scheduled for the beginning of the new year, but had to be canceled. Thanks to Jeffrey's persistence and encouragement, the tour was now on again, to start early in June.

Until then, Marvin and his musicians—keyboard player William Bryant, guitarist Gordon Banks, drummer Bugsy Wilcox, and bass player Frank Blair—concentrated on the new *Love Man* album. There was one hitch: Marvin had a change of mind about the project's theme. He didn't want to do another album that had him coming across as a "love man." He said, "I've already done that to death. It's time to grow up and move on, time to get back to more serious themes and put them to music." He originally retitled the new album *In Our Lifetime?* Most of the songs Marvin had written for *Love Man* were retitled and, with new lyrics, were retained for the new album, and became side one. Side two was made up of songs specifically written for *In Our Lifetime?*

When the album was released, the question mark in the title had been dropped. Marvin was furious, but he calmed down quickly when he was promised a correction on the next printing. It became only a mild irritation once he began rehearsals for the upcoming Heavy Love Affair tour, a title he had taken from one of the songs in his *In Our Lifetime?* album. June was fast approaching.

Despite all that had happened in Marvin's life during his exile in Hawaii, he was not the basket case he'd been made out to be when he left for London. Without question, he was nervous as he prepared to leave for the first leg of his tour. He had learned that Jan had filed legal papers to regain custody of Bubby. He knew there was a good chance he would be served when he landed in Los Angeles to change planes for London. At the last minute, he booked his flight through San Francisco.

There was another worry: Bubby didn't have a passport. According to Marvin, he somehow managed to get him through by covering him with a blanket. That wasn't all. Ahead were a series of tour stops and live audiences, which brought back all the terrifying thoughts of performing again. He loved his European fans, but would they accept him after all these years?

Arriving in London, Marvin and little Bubby were met by banks of waiting photographers. Marvin looked awful, tired and thin. The past months in Hawaii had taken a toll on him, but he managed a smile for the crowd.

A VIP suite was awaiting at the Britannia Hotel on Grosvenor Square, in Mayfair. With hardly any time to rest after the long overseas flight, he was back in the swim again, rehearsing and being fitted for his stage outfit: an English-cut black suit, white shirt, and knitted cap. On June 13th—a Friday—he stepped onto the stage at the Royal Albert Hall to a rousing ovation. Admittedly nervous, he told the loving opening-night crowd, "We finally made it. We've had a few problems, but what can I tell you? We like to keep you guessing." His last words were a reference to his earlier cancellation, and his "will he–won't he appear" reputation. As far as the audience was concerned, he was with them now, and that seemed to be all that mattered. They laughed at his little attempt at humor, clapped and hollered as he began to sing, and he soon began to settle down. By the end of the evening's performance, after nearly two hours onstage, he appeared to be his usual people-pleasing self. But he gave no encore, despite the screaming, stomping pleas of the audience. Instead, he brought Bubby onstage to share in the ovation.

The crowd didn't want to let him go. They loved the concert; in their eyes he could do no wrong. The critics weren't quite in unison, however. He got good-to-excellent reviews for the most part, but there were several critics who criticized his sexual references and gestures. Looking back on that night, whatever they objected to was tame compared to what was to come.

Little has been written about Marvin's visit to England in 1980, except to say that he fell in with "a bad crowd." A bad crowd? Hardly. Marvin met and associated with some unsavory characters wherever he went, and that probably happened in England, too. But the overwhelming majority of people who were close to him during that visit were the most beautiful, warm, and caring individuals imaginable. In London, and in all of Europe, for that matter, Marvin was respected as an artist, not because of how many records he had sold over the past few months. The fact that he hadn't had a hit for some time didn't matter at all to his European fans.

During Marvin's stay in London, he was introduced to many important people, both in the music business and in high society. It was at the opening of Cheeks, a nightclub in the East End, that he met Lady Edith Foxwell, a member of the British aristocracy and a prominent figure in London's social circles. Granted the title "Lady" by King George VI in 1947, she was the daughter of the second son of the ninth earl of Cavan. Her mother, an American, was a Whitney, one of the families who built the railroads in America. Educated by governesses, she became one of England's most high-spirited debutantes. In 1940, she married British screenwriter Ivan Foxwell, which led her to organizing many of his film premieres, as well as royal premieres. Following their divorce in 1975, Lady Edith took to the nightlife at disco-dancing clubs, wearing figure-hugging, gold-lamé outfits.

As Lady Edith began devoting much of her time to charity work, she soon became a fixture in the London music scene. Her parties, particularly at the Embassy Club, were the talk of the town. An attractive, vivacious woman in her early sixties when Marvin arrived in London for his 1980 tour, she was always exquisitely groomed. Marvin could hardly stop talking about her auburn hair, which she wore in a shoulder-length pageboy. "I don't know how she does it," he'd say, "but there's never a strand out of place."

Lady Edith had a 16th-century Elizabethan manor house at Sherston, in Wiltshire, as well as a luxurious flat in London. By the time Marvin sent for me to come to England, he was spending most of his days and nights at Sherston.

My first day in London had me feeling like royalty myself, and unprepared for storybook living. I was met at the airport by Marvin and Lady Edith, then driven in a limousine to Sherston, where I got the grand tour. The manor house and grounds were even more impressive than Marvin had described, and he was never one to underestimate anything.

Once my eyes had adjusted to all the fancy trappings, it was time to rest, then dress for a formal dinner at the home of Lady Edith's close friend, Sherrill Chidiac. At 7 P.M., we were back in the limousine, on our way to Kensington Park Gardens in London.

After seeing Lady Edith's estate, I thought I had seen everything, but when the butler opened the door to us at Sherrill's four-story Edwardian home, I'm sure I gasped. I had never seen columns inside a

house before, ceilings so high, mirrors so huge, such intricate mold-
ing or furniture that was inlaid with silver, mother-of-pearl, and ivory.
What next? I wondered. I half expected to see a man hitting a huge
gong, like at the beginning of J. Arthur Rank movies. For a guy from
Simple City, this was the closest I'd ever come to a palace. I was awe-
struck, but Marvin took it all in stride. He was certainly a lot cooler
than me.

We were graciously welcomed by Sherrill, a soft-spoken, beautiful young woman dressed in shimmering satin. She looked so glamorous, I must have gasped again. As Sherrill remembers, "Frankie was
so wide-eyed, so speechless when we first met. Later he told me he
must have made a fool of himself, but that wasn't the case at all. He
just seemed a bit overwhelmed, which endeared him to me." Marvin,
of course, had been to Motown's charm school, where something obviously had made a lasting impression. As for Lady Edith, well, she had
been to Sherrill's various parties, charity events, and fund-raisers. "Being in London," says Sherrill, "my place was more convenient than
Lady Edith's country estate, and more suited to entertaining than her
flat in the city. Lady Edith and I had mutual friends in business, pol-
itics, and the arts."

At dinner, which was very formal, I embarrassed myself again. I
was used to a simple table setting with one spoon, one fork, and one
knife, and it didn't matter which side of the plate they were on. At
Sherrill's, the silverware—real silver—fanned out on both sides of the
plates. There were at least three of everything. It was the same with
the dishes—little ones, big ones, some on top of each other. And the
glasses, or rather, the crystal, were spread out in bunches before me. I
was so busy watching Lady Edith and Sherrill to see what they were
using, I hardly had time to eat. I may have been awkward, but that
evening was a good lesson for living at Sherston.

Marvin and I were totally pampered at Sherston, but Marvin received most of the attention. Lady Edith, who had a weakness for
young black men, was especially taken with him. And while Marvin,

at forty-one, was not that young, he was at least 20 years younger than Lady Edith, and he was special. She had pictures of him all over the estate, even at her London flat. For the first time, she allowed her famous baby-grand piano, said to have been played by royalty, to leave her study. She had it pushed outside onto a grassy area near the pool so that Marvin could start composing again.

It wasn't long before items began appearing in the newspaper columns, spreading word about Marvin and Lady Edith hobnobbing around town together. The writers took to calling her "Queen of the nightlife ... out on her strawberry daiquiri–fueled forays into café society." Lady Edith and Marvin even joked about getting married. "Then I'll be Lady Gaye," she quipped, loving the sound of that.

A different sort of romance came into my life. It started in Marvin's dressing room, which was crowded with well-wishers before one of his shows. I was sitting between three ladies, bored to death, when the door opened and in walked a tall blonde with a really great tan. She was carrying a big box, which she handed to Marvin. He opened it and pulled out a Hawaiian orchid lei and other colorful souvenirs from the islands. As he put the lei around his neck, he smiled, called me over, and said, "Let me introduce my brother, Frankie. Stick with him. He'll take good care of you." Then Marvin left. He had to get dressed for the show.

Her name was Irene Duncan, and she was Scottish. She had just returned from Hawaii with gifts for Marvin. Irene remembers, "I was in Honolulu on a business vacation, working in promotion for a timeshare company. On my last night there I went out to dinner with a few locals, and when I told them I was returning home to London, where I was living then, they got all excited, not because I was leaving but because they knew Marvin had just left the islands to start his tour of England. 'Oh, we've got to send him some love,' they squealed. They wanted to put together a box filled with little gifts from Hawaii. I agreed to do it, but how would I find him? And how would I get it to him? They said they knew some of Marvin's people. If I went to the Apollo Theater, I'd get in. No trouble.

"I did get past the guards at the theater easily. I guess they figured someone with a brogue and a tan had to be special. Next thing I knew, I was being escorted to Marvin's dressing room, which was crowded with people. The first person I saw was Frankie, who was sitting on a sofa surrounded by girls. I thought he was Marvin at first, but I was led across the room to another man who looked like Marvin. Then the guard said, 'Mr. Gaye, this woman has a package for you.' Marvin opened the box, thanked me, and called to Frankie."

As I walked toward Marvin to meet Irene, my legs felt rubbery. She was tall, trim, and tanned, with sun-bleached hair. She took my breath away.

I thought I had lost her when we heard the last call before showtime. Everyone was leaving the dressing room to get to their seats, but I had to lag behind to see that everything was secure and locked up. When I looked around, Irene was going off with Omar, a London couturier with deep pockets full of cash, taking her away to watch the show with him. They were heading for the elevator, which would take them down to the main floor. I started to run after her, but it was too late.

"Frankie got to the elevator just as the doors closed," says Irene. "Then I heard Omar say, 'I have seats in the audience. I want you to sit with me.' I had only just met Frankie, but there was a connection between us, a spark, right off. He was so soft-spoken and warm."

I didn't know where Irene was, and I was growing more and more upset. As Marvin came onstage, I moved to the wings to look out into the audience, but I couldn't find her.

"I could see Frankie in the wings from where I was sitting," Irene recalls, "and I wondered how I could get backstage again to be with him, or even just to say goodbye to him. I told Omar I had to leave, then made my way to the security door. The guard had that 'Oh, no, not you again,' look on his face when I told him I was really supposed to be backstage, but I landed in the audience by mistake. He didn't believe me. 'Sure, lady,' he snickered, and started to close the door. I persisted until he finally said, 'I'll take you back there, but if Frankie Gaye doesn't know you, or claims he's never seen you before, you're not even getting back to see the show. You're out of here!'

"He took me backstage, and with each step I was getting more nervous. Would Frankie remember me? I wondered. Would he want to remember me? The guard and I were only a few yards away when Frankie turned and saw me. His face lit up, and he called out my name. With that, the guard left, and as he did, Frankie put his arm around my shoulder. Onstage, Marvin was singing 'Distant Lover.' "

I barely heard Marvin's performance that night. There was only the voice in my head telling me I had to wait nearly 40 years, and go to Europe, to fall in love.

12

Marvin made history in London—not all of it good. He played eight dates in Great Britain, then after side trips to the Netherlands and Switzerland for concerts in four cities, he returned to England. He still had one more concert: a Royal Gala Charity Show at Lakeside Country Club in Surrey. A sister of Queen Elizabeth II, Princess Margaret, was a friend of Lady Edith's and a fan of Marvin's; she had agreed to attend as the guest of honor, which made the event even more important. The keepsake program, with Marvin on the cover, featured Princess Margaret on the inside, with a full-page portrait.

Marvin had especially looked forward to this concert, because it benefited the children of London's Docklands Settlement. Tickets weren't cheap. He knew his appearance there would generate a lot of money for a good cause.

On the day of the concert, Marvin and his musicians, along with everyone else connected with the tour, were in London, waiting for Jeffrey Kruger, the tour promoter, to show up with the payroll and airline tickets to get back to America. The arranged time came and went, but Jeffrey never arrived. Marvin had me call him, which I did a number of times, but he was either "unavailable" or "not at his desk." As showtime neared, Marvin threw up his hands.

It was getting late, and he insisted we make tracks for Surrey, about a half-hour ride outside London.

By the time we arrived at Lakeside Country Club, the concert was nearly over, and Princess Margaret had gone. Marvin went on anyway, but the papers headlined his "snub" of the princess. Said one report, "The Lakeside concert was a great honor for the singer [Marvin Gaye], and we were totally astonished when he blew it. There is no real satisfactory reason we can offer for an excuse. It is quite inexcusable!"

The truth is, contrary to reports that he was down with drugs, Marvin made every effort to perform, and he did. Because of protocol, however, Princess Margaret had to leave early. Lady Edith Foxwell rose to defend Marvin. On his behalf, she announced, "Given the circumstances, Marvin Gaye did not have to attend, but he did anyway. Unfortunately, he arrived later than his scheduled start. The princess had to leave and that made him very upset. He didn't mean to be rude. He was extremely depressed." As it turned out, according to Lady Edith, the princess was not as perturbed as the press had led everyone to believe. Disappointed, but not enough to create such a fuss.

Marvin knew the negative press would leave a sour taste in the mouths of his British fans, people he truly loved and respected. He blamed Jeffrey for that. Marvin believed Jeffrey was withholding money and airline tickets until after the final concert, to make sure everyone showed up on time. It was a ploy, Marvin felt certain; he was being manipulated down to the wire. He actually didn't mind; he had decided not to go back to the States anyway. "A voice inside keeps telling me to stay away," he told me. "No telling what the government guys have waiting for me." He knew it was trouble.

Following the last concert, Marvin had no commitments, no tour schedule, no recordings in the offing. He tried to arrange another British tour, but coming on the heels of the last one, there was little interest. To make matters worse, Jan had flown to London, hoping to salvage their marriage and take Bubby home with her. Marvin wanted the relationship to work, and for a brief moment it seemed they would get back together again. Then the fireworks started all over. Jan left, leaving Bubby behind. She would fly back and forth over the coming months to see Marvin, but the results were always the same.

With no work and no prospects in sight, Marvin began sliding downhill again. I had gone home, leaving only a few members of Marvin's entourage still hanging around, but their ranks were getting even thinner. His only positive was Lady Edith, who offered some stability and advice, quiet weekends in the country, and rousing evenings on the town. Financially, Marvin couldn't keep up with Lady Edith, but she didn't expect him to. What little money he had came from her and from the slim advances he received from the coffers of Motown UK (United Kingdom).

During the week, Marvin was staying in a rented flat in Bedford Gardens, awaiting the arrival of a Dutch girl named Eugenie Vis, whom he was bringing over from Amsterdam to be Bubby's live-in nanny—and perhaps more. He had met Eugenie through his bass player, Frank Blair, after one of their concerts in the Netherlands. An attractive country girl in her mid-twenties, she had never heard of Marvin until she saw him perform. But she must have liked what she saw; Marvin certainly did. When he asked her to work for him, she said she'd give it a try. She remained with Marvin throughout most of his stay in Europe. Shortly after Eugenie's arrival, Marvin, Bubby, and his new nanny moved to another flat on Boxer Road.

Marvin's inactive professional life was getting to him. With nothing else to keep his mind occupied, he dwelled on his troubles at home. Once again, he began to rely heavily on drugs to erase the ugly thoughts that haunted him. By the time he met Freddy Cousaert, he felt his career was over and that he would never sing again. Bogged down by his personal problems, singing had become a chore. If the act of singing hadn't been stressful enough, he also had to deal with the business end of things. The way things were going, he couldn't face that anymore.

Freddy Cousaert was a great admirer of Marvin and his music. He was also fully aware of Marvin's many difficulties. A boxing promoter without any real experience in show business, Freddy was a positive thinker, strong on inspiration. It was a relief for Marvin to meet someone who didn't want something from him and didn't only want to talk about "the business." It was good, too, to meet a fellow boxing aficionado, especially the man who had brought one of Marvin's idols, Muhammed Ali, to Belgium for a fight. Marvin didn't open up to many people right off, but once he heard Freddy relate his Ali story, he had to tell about his failed involvement in boxing. And he couldn't wait to describe his own time in the ring with the heavyweight champ at a charity event held in downtown Los Angeles, at the Olympic Auditorium, for Marvin's pet project, Save the Children. Marvin was thrilled to be able to get in the ring with Ali. There were so many things he had admired about the fighter: his stand on Vietnam, his brash attitude, and his ability to promote himself, among many other things. Ali was the champ that Marvin had always wanted to be.

The evening was an all-star happening. Besides Marvin, Ali had agreed to go a round with Richard Pryor; Sammy Davis, Jr.; and Burt Young, who had played the frustrated brother-in-law to Sylvester Stallone in the *Rocky* series of movies. Everyone knew how they were going to handle their time in the ring with Ali. It was all a setup for laughs, which would have them running, jumping, and clowning around. Not Marvin. He had to take his one chance at the champ by training seriously. "I'm going to knock him out," Marvin had boldly predicted beforehand. He'd even come up with some serious threads to parade in, for his entrance into the ring.

There were lots of laughs before Ali and Marvin climbed into the ring, with Ali coaching Marvin by saying, "Now don't hit me too hard or try to show off." Those remarks had Marvin responding with, "Go ahead, hit me with your best shot. Don't just try to make it look good!" Wearing his classy robe, Marvin might have come across as a pro, but once he took it off he turned into a string bean, his long arms flailing, hitting nothing but air. But Ali kept missing too, on purpose, which made Marvin mad. Ali landed only one light jab, and even that had Marvin bent over, staggering. "You okay?" Ali asked, grabbing Marvin to keep him from falling. It was over almost before it started, but the crowd had a great time.

Freddy and Marvin traded boxing stories, enjoying every minute of their time together. Before their meeting was over, Freddy sensed a spirited potential that still existed in Marvin, and Marvin felt uplifted just being in the company of his newfound friend. When Freddy offered Marvin, Eugenie, and Bubby a place to stay in his Belgian hometown, Marvin couldn't refuse.

Marvin didn't really know where he was going. "I left that in the hands of God," he told me later. It didn't matter where Freddy was taking him; Belgium seemed as good a place as any. For Marvin, Belgium represented an escape to another world, a distant place that had nothing to do with singing or with being Marvin Gaye.

13

*E*arly in the morning on February 15th, 1981, Freddy Cousaert picked up Marvin, Bubby, and Eugenie at their Boxer Road flat and drove to the seaport town of Dover. There they boarded a Sealink ferry that would take them across the Strait of Dover to the harbor city of Ostend, Belgium. It was a chilly trip in the damp air.

To Marvin, the ferry didn't seem to be making much headway as it skimmed across the dark water. On this gray day, the coastlines of France and Belgium were fogged in. With little to see or do, Marvin jumped when he was invited to join the captain for drinks on the bridge. Freddy tagged along. He felt that Marvin was now his responsibility, and he wanted to keep an eye on him. No telling what the captain might say that could possibly upset Marvin.

A brisk, cold wind was blowing as the passengers stepped from the ferry onto the dock at Ostend. Marvin later commented that he had never felt such raw weather, but his memory was short. He had forgotten the freezing winters we had lived through when we were growing up in Washington, D.C.

From the waterfront at Ostend, Freddy led Marvin, Bubby, and Eugenie to a small boarding house at 77 Rue Promenade, just a block from the beach. Freddy's wife, Lilliane, a joyous woman, was waiting for them with open arms. She had already prepared a room on the fifth floor for Freddy's guests and had a hot meal simmering on the stove.

The boarding house was owned by Freddy and managed by his wife. They lived in the basement apartment, along with their two young daughters. Lilliane had told them that a new playmate would be arriving, and they had eagerly anticipated meeting Bubby. Freddy seemed happy too, now that Marvin was safely in tow. As for Marvin, he was simply relieved to be warm again and on dry land.

From the moment she first saw Marvin, Lilliane was concerned with his appearance. She felt that he looked thin, exhausted, and stressed out. "And," she observed, "there was a sadness in his eyes." Her husband told her not to worry. He had big plans for Marvin that would turn his life and career around. Freddy was not easily discouraged. He had tremendous confidence in himself and in Marvin. He was quite an optimist.

Following Marvin's arrival in Ostend, he and Freddy spent their days together talking endlessly. Marvin was never a person who could talk easily about himself and his troubles, especially to someone he had known only a short time. The really personal things, the hurtful things, he kept inside. I was one of the few exceptions who heard it all, even his darkest moments, when he talked about suicide. But in the hours Marvin spent with Freddy, he began to learn more about him too. Freddy's kindness, his seemingly genuine sincerity, and his glowing optimism had Marvin opening up. Freddy's string of successes as a boxing promoter, concert promoter, talent scout (he once owned a disco in Ostend), and tour manager didn't hurt either. Within days, Marvin thought of Freddy as a true friend, someone he could trust. Trust was *it* to Marvin. Trust meant everything. In the beginning of his career, when Marvin first started singing, he trusted almost everyone. Now he trusted very few people, but Freddy was one of them.

Freddy believed in Marvin too. In fact, Marvin had long been his hero. More than getting Marvin into a new, less pressured environment, away from the demands and temptations of big-city life, he sincerely wanted to help Marvin in every possible way. Marvin's body, mind, and spirit were his first priorities. From there, Freddy told him, they would talk about the future, which included more than Marvin the person. Freddy wanted to be Marvin's manager. But that would never happen unless Marvin "got his act together," in the personal sense.

Marvin was all too ready to let Freddy take over. Singing, being onstage, and making records were no longer of interest to him, and hadn't been since the end of the tour in England. For now, Marvin was simply content to meet Freddy's friends and other locals, who were warm, kind, and gentle, and who were unaffected by fame or the color of a person's skin. Except for occasional sports teams and musicians who passed through town, Marvin was the only black that many of them had ever seen in person. It didn't even matter that he couldn't speak their language. Freddy was usually there to speak for him, whether it was Flemish, French, or Italian. When he wasn't there, Marvin knew his smile was worth a thousand words, at least. In time, he began to feel like he belonged.

Marvin loved hanging out with Freddy and Lilliane. More than anything, he loved playing with Bubby and the Cousaerts's two daughters. His time with the children—running, playing games, and skateboarding—was only a warm-up for the more strenuous activities that Freddy was setting up for him.

Marvin had always enjoyed the outdoors and sports, and like most everything he became fanatical about, it wasn't long before he couldn't get enough of Freddy's new routine for him. Early mornings found him working out in a gym, shadowboxing, cycling, and running laps. Soon the mornings stretched into afternoons, then early evenings. He even began to eat properly.

When Marvin wasn't in the gym, he could be found hiking, pitching horseshoes, shooting hoops, or taking long walks along the water's edge on Ostend's strip of sandy beach. He walked alone as the sun was setting on cloudless days, in the quiet of late evenings, in the rain. The blustery weather didn't faze him now. Bundled up in a heavy wool jacket, with a knit cap protecting his head, he was in a zone all his own, his mind moving in new directions. As Marvin worked to cleanse and rebuild his body, his confidence began to return, and it grew stronger with each new day.

Marvin loved the beach. It was the perfect opposite of the stuffy, often overheated, gym where he worked out. He would often stand looking out to sea, facing the wind, telling himself, "It's working. It's working." I once asked him, "What's working?" All he'd say was, "I'm breezing the old ways off me."

The beach was only a few steps away from Marvin's new seafront apartment. The bigger living quarters, along with a nice advance, were all part of Freddy's plan to rebuild a new Marvin Gaye, mentally and physically, in order to promote his comeback. Marvin was once again thinking along those lines too. He was drug-free and his fears were fading, much like the waves that lapped up on the shore, then disappeared.

Marvin was so full of changes, so many different emotions. Before he'd left for Hawaii, he had said to me, "What did I give them this time, five years? I may stay away for a while, but when I come back, I come back strong."

During one of Marvin's "disappearances"—I forget exactly what drove him away that time—I said to him, "You can't just run away from everything and everyone."

"Why can't I?" he replied.

"Because too many people depend on you." It was true. From the moment Marvin started making money, he had felt responsible to others, more than to himself, and that was one of his great weaknesses, his Achilles' heel.

He looked down sheepishly and shook his head. "Aw, I've made up my mind. I'm gone."

"Gone? How can you relax when all these people count on you? They're your friends, family, coworkers."

He started to walk away, then stopped. "No matter where I go," he said quietly, "it's always somebody."

I felt like a dog putting more pressure on him, but I couldn't help myself. I was only trying to keep him from withdrawing into a deeper funk, which might have been even more harmful to him. He wouldn't admit it at the time, but I knew he wouldn't give in to his pressures. He *had* to keep going. He *had* to come back. It was his built-in determination to be the best that would motivate him.

I honestly believe that Marvin carried these thoughts with him always, and that coming to Ostend and associating himself with Freddy Cousaert was the beginning of his latest comeback. Marvin had always fought back. No matter what he said when he was at his lowest, he always managed to somehow turn his life around.

Marvin was spoiled and stubborn, same as he had been from the time we were growing up. As a kid, he knew what he wanted and he went after it. He usually got what he wanted too, and for the most part, he came out a winner.

The melodies Marvin had written during his visits to Lady Edith's, in Sherston, began running through his head again, as he worked out and walked in Ostend. They were not complete songs, only a few bars here and there from different pieces, but the melodic lines were strong enough to get him back to a piano. He talked again of a tour and of recording a new album, but not with Motown. He knew Diana Ross had recently cut her ties with the label. The time had finally come for him to cut loose too. Marvin let it be known that he was thinking of getting back to work. His comments began to create a buzz, not only with the public, but within the music industry. What he had in mind this time no one really knew, but he had been out of sight way too long—nothing new for Marvin—and the response to his anticipated return, despite his many problems, was generally positive.

Over the years, Marvin had been in touch with various recording companies, including Arista and Electra/Asylum. But in the spring of 1981, shortly after Marvin ended his long relationship with Motown, he began making phone calls. Odell Brown, Marvin's keyboard player, had once worked with Johnny Nash and Minnie Riperton at

Columbia Records, a subsidiary of CBS. Odell's former connection there, and the fact that Michael Jackson had jumped from Motown to CBS several years earlier, had Marvin thinking that CBS might be the place for him. He contacted Larkin Arnold, who was vice president of CBS and head of black music for the label. Hearing that Marvin was available, planning a new tour, and physically healthy again, had Arnold interested. It would be nearly a year before negotiations were completed with CBS, but once they were and contracts were signed, Marvin came away with a sweet deal. Besides being guaranteed a considerable advance per album, CBS agreed to pay off many of Marvin's debts and to clear him with the IRS.

Until the arrangements with CBS were fully signed and sealed, and the first of the advances were received, Marvin needed some spending money. Freddy Cousaert set up and began to promote a two-week tour of England, which would take him back across the English Channel from June 13th through July 1st of 1981. The tour was called A Heavy Love Affair Tour 1981, the "Heavy Love Affair" in the title coming from the song of the same name in Marvin's *In Our Lifetime?* album.

As a goodwill warm-up for the tour, Freddy exposed Marvin to audiences for the first time in many months. Marvin sang to a crowd at a local gym, before townspeople who could never afford to pay to hear him. He appeared at soccer games, where he was presented at halftime. He taped a television program for local showing and for syndication elsewhere in Europe, called "Marvin Gaye—Transit Ostend"; he was even introduced to Prince Charles of Belgium. A photo of Marvin and Prince Charles together was featured in the Heavy Love Affair tour program, along with a quote. Marvin said, "The prince and I got to be good friends. I stayed at his place for a few days, on and off. He's a great artist. He would paint a lot while I was there. He's a marvelous man and I love him dearly." Later, when we were alone, Marvin told me, "The prince is an outcast in his family because he likes black music, and who knows what else. His brothers and sisters do not appreciate that sort of thing."

Just before the start of the tour, Marvin had me flown to London to work with him. There were fewer familiar faces this time, since the tour group was cut way back. No hangers-on, thanks to Freddy, who tried his best to make it all happen with as few expenses as possible. Marvin's keyboardist, Odell Brown, was there, as well as his guitarist, Gordon Banks, who was there to lead the small band. The only other person I knew from before was Lady Edith Foxwell, who volunteered to help with promotion and to encourage Marvin whenever his nerves began to flair up. Lady Edith and Freddy didn't get along at all, mainly because they each had their own way of doing things. But she was much too important within the London music scene for him to get in her way.

Lady Edith caused me an anxious moment, however. She wouldn't tell me how it happened, only that it was "a quirky little accident," but she broke her elbow shortly before Marvin's opening night. She tried to laugh it off, even though she was in obvious pain as I drove her to the hospital. Lady Edith always drew attention wherever she went. But at the hospital, all eyes were on me; everyone thought *I* was Marvin. I tried to explain, which was a waste of time, and Lady Edith was no help. She simply stood by laughing at me. "It was terribly amusing," she told Marvin when we met him later. He thought it was funny too.

Marvin's opening performance at the Apollo Theater had his audience begging for more. Freddy was pacing, afraid no one would show up because of the stormy weather, but by showtime the theater was packed. Marvin was relaxed, he looked good, and he sounded sensational. He sang what everyone wanted to hear, long versions of his old favorites, with a few medleys in the mix too. He even threw in new versions of "What's Going On," "Distant Lover," and "Inner City Blues."

The surprise of the evening was Stevie Wonder, who came onstage to sing "I Heard It Through the Grapevine" with Marvin. It was a great evening. Marvin seemed to be his old self again, low-key, sexy, and having fun. It was good to see him smiling and to feel his renewed enthusiasm. He was loving life again.

The remaining dates on the tour never reached the same high, mainly because the receipts fell below expectations. Everyone tried to make each stop a success but the feeling was, aside from London, Marvin probably should have performed in other big European cities, where his fans hadn't seen him within the past year.

Once the tour ended, Marvin was on his way back to Ostend. I didn't want to linger in England, either! I had a "performance" of my own to attend in Los Angeles. With no more than a quick good-bye, Marvin and I went our separate ways.

Irene and I were getting married. We had set July 4th as the day, and all the arrangements had been made. The fourth was my choice, because I knew that it was a date I would never forget as our anniversary. Having grown up in Scotland, Irene knew nothing about our American holiday. So that evening, in our hotel suite after the ceremony, I pulled up the blinds and we stood looking out at the city lights. We were high up on the top floor of the hotel, which gave us a great view.

At nine o'clock the sky exploded with color, fireworks everywhere, as the nighttime display went on and on. Irene was thrilled; she had never seen anything like it. "Oh, that is so beautiful," she sighed.

I looked at her dreamily and said, "It's all for you, dear."

She nearly melted thinking I had arranged the spectacular fireworks show to celebrate our wedding. She eventually found out that I had nothing to do with it, but not before I scampered down to the lobby the next morning to buy up all the newspapers. She wasn't mad. She simply smiled and said, "From now on, all of America will be celebrating our anniversary."

It wasn't too many months later that Marvin was calling me back across the Atlantic, this time to Belgium. "Bring your bride along with you," he said. His musicians were on their way too, along with Harvey Fuqua and his girlfriend Marilyn Freeman. Marvin and

Harvey hadn't talked in nearly five years. Now they would be working together again.

Once we arrived in Ostend, Irene and I were driven to Freddy Cousaert's boarding house on Rue Promenade. We unpacked and settled into our room before we discovered we had no bathroom, no shower, no toilet. All that was down the hall, to be shared with everyone else on our floor. It took some getting used to, but we soon adjusted. In a pinch, if the facilities were occupied we could usually find another one empty on the floor above or below. I could understand why Marvin was so much happier in his seafront apartment, with his own private head.

Since I had last seen Marvin, Jan and Nona had visited Ostend. Even though he and Jan were now divorced, he was hoping things would work out for the two of them, bringing his family together again. It didn't happen that way. Jan wanted only to work out an agreement over the children. According to Marvin, their reunion "wasn't pretty." Even though they were still soul mates, he said, despite all that had happened between them, they fought, then fought some more. Jan returned to California with Nona and Bubby. Eugenie was gone, too. Her leaving had nothing to do with Bubby's departure. Marvin had discovered that she'd had an affair with one of his band members from the Heavy Love Affair tour.

Marvin missed Mother and his children, but Europe had become his home. Although he had little money, he admitted that he felt "wealthy in soul" and that he had finally become "the artist I always wanted to be." He had left all his pressures at home, halfway around the world. Now, despite his new happiness, he was calling them back again to this quiet, faraway, and secluded seafront town. I wondered what would come along with them.

Marvin was now spending most of his time working on songs for his new CBS album, and Freddy was pushing him to make music. Marvin had set up a studio in his apartment, and it was loaded with equipment bought for him by CBS. He also had a drum machine that Stevie Wonder had given him when they saw each other in June. For the most part, Marvin worked alone, writing down whatever popped into his head. It didn't matter if they were disconnected bars of music, lingering melodies born on Lady Edith's piano, bits of lyrics, even random words that he thought would work as titles.

Marvin once said, "There's always a song in the air." If his songs were plucked from the air, they had their roots in life, his life, whatever was going on with him at the time. Some of those songs took off, others didn't. His problem now was in trying to recapture his past successes. He was especially trying to steer away from another concept album on the order of *What's Going On*. He had done that, he said, or so he was told. Now the heat was on him to come up with something new, and just as important, something commercial. The trouble was, Marvin didn't think in a commercial way.

Years later, a writer from England asked me about Marvin during that creative time in Belgium. By then I'd had time to reflect on it, and I told him that I honestly believed, and still do, that period in Marvin's life set the course for his final days. That period was when he got away from his true calling as a songwriter with a social conscience, and an awareness of his spirituality, and he turned back into a black sex god. It was always a struggle for Marvin between the truths of his upbringing and the world out there. In wanting to please the powers of the music industry, and *needing* to please, he felt he had no choice but to sing sexy songs. "That's where the money is," Marvin was told. "That's what your fans expect from you."

Marvin actually had little choice in the matter. In striking a deal with CBS he did something he swore he would never do again, not after he had fought so hard for his independence at Motown. He turned artistic control over to his new label.

As soon as Marvin had a few songs, he felt he was ready to start recording. It didn't matter if they were songs without lyrics, or if the titles meant nothing at this point and might eventually be scrapped. He just wanted to get back into a studio. Freddy had set him up at Studio Katy, a small operation outside Brussels, in the town of Ohaine. Working with Marvin were his keyboardist, Odell Brown;

drummer William Bryant; and guitarists Danny Esters, Donni Hagen, and local guitarist Danny Bosaert. Gordon Banks, the talented guitarist who had married our baby sister, "Sweetsie," was the music director.

The basic tracks for four songs were cut in Ohaine. One of them was without a title or lyrics; it was strictly instrumental. Marvin loved the song, but Odell Brown had written it, and Marvin's contract with CBS required that he write all the songs for the new album. It was up to Marvin to at least coauthor the number, and he had nothing in mind for it, not even a thematic idea. He also had to come up with the remaining songs for the album.

Several months passed, and Odell's song was still without a title or lyrics. It was at that point Freddy received a call from Curtis Shaw, Marvin's attorney, who was in Los Angeles. "A writer named David Ritz is on his way to Ostend," Shaw told Freddy. "He wants to interview Marvin for a book he's writing, a dual biography of Marvin and Diana Ross."

"No way, not now," Marvin exploded when Freddy relayed Shaw's message. "Not a good time. Stop him. Don't let him come through!"

Freddy met David Ritz at the train station in Ostend, but he wouldn't take him to see Marvin or tell him where Marvin was staying. "He's too busy," he told Ritz. "His album is due and he can't be bothered."

Ritz found Marvin, which wasn't difficult. If Marvin wasn't the only black person in Ostend, he was certainly one of the very few, and word had gotten around town that the American singer Marvin Gaye was living there. Ritz showed up unannounced and uninvited at Marvin's waterfront apartment, and Marvin, who was not in the greatest mood that day, surprisingly opened the door wide. I was sitting with Marvin at the time, and when I heard the visitor's name, I waited for the fireworks. There weren't any; Marvin remained strangely calm. As I shifted in my chair, Marvin motioned for me to stay. I wasn't about to leave.

Marvin's privacy had been violated. How would he respond to the questions that were about to come from this man? I wondered. Ritz explained who he was and why he had come to Belgium. Then the questions began. Marvin didn't say anything to write home about. His words came out but they were guarded. It was all rather businesslike.

At one point, Marvin began to loosen up. As happy as he had been in Ostend, he spoke of wanting to find an island somewhere, leaning back and forgetting about his troubled life. "Success don't bring you nothing but heartache and grief," he said quietly. "Everything I've tried to do to help people somehow turns on you. Then it comes back to you in evil ways. Does everyone have an ulterior motive?" Marvin gave Ritz a long look and the room went quiet. Then Marvin said, "I want you to hear something." He reached for one of the tapes from the recording sessions in Ohaine. It was the Odell Brown track.

The rhythm of the funky, reggae-styled music filled the room. Marvin played the tape over and over, saying, "I pray to God it's going to be a hit" more than once. He still hadn't written any words to put to it. They just wouldn't come to him, he said. At that point, Ritz commented, "Not only are you sexy, your music is healing." That was it. Ritz's few words were said casually and in passing, but they stayed in Marvin's head.

Days later, after Ritz had departed, Marvin said to me, "That's pretty nice. Sexual healing." Something had clicked. On the *Midnight Love* album, David Ritz was acknowledged for creating the title of the song, "Sexual Healing," even though he hadn't even put the two words together. Perhaps Marvin was displaying hidden psychic powers when he laid his soul bare for Ritz.

When Freddy Cousaert learned that David Ritz had seen Marvin despite being told to stay away, he was irate. When he learned that Ritz was being credited with the title, he thought it was an overly generous gesture. Marvin's musicians treated it as a joke. They weren't even aware Ritz had been in town, if only briefly. I knew because I was there that day. I also knew how much, or rather how little, Ritz had contributed. (A year after Ritz's visit to Ostend, he sued Marvin for $15 million in damages for failing to credit him as a lyricist of the song, with CBS Records named as codefendant. When Marvin first heard that Ritz wanted credit, he shook his head and said, "The guy's got to be kidding. Just tell him to sue me. It'll up the sales of his book." The book, however, which was rushed out shortly after Marvin's death, was no longer a dual biography. It was all Marvin, all the way. As for the lawsuit, it caused Marvin great distress, even though it was ultimately dropped in court, and for good reason.)

The recording sessions in Ohaine were nearly completed when Marvin received a call from Diana Ross. She was in Brussels for a concert to promote "Muscles," a new single from her latest album, *Silk Electric.* Marvin and Freddy drove to Brussels to see Diana, not knowing what to expect. During an earlier concert in London, before a huge crowd at Wembley Stadium, she all but cracked when the sound system went bad. Stopping the show, she screamed at the sound crew, then kicked one of the sound monitors off the stage. When the London critics blasted her, Diana apologized by saying, "I think I handled it badly, but I'm not perfect."

She made up for London in Brussels, according to Marvin. He went for one performance and stayed for two. The first night, he received a standing ovation as he walked down the aisle to his seat. "I never expected that," he said, beaming. The next night Diana coaxed him up to the stage to cheers and screams, which lasted throughout their unrehearsed duet. Marvin admitted that being onstage with her again was not only thrilling, but emotional for him.

Diana must have enjoyed it too for she canceled whatever she had planned for later that evening to go with Marvin and Freddy to the studio in Ohaine to hear his new recordings. By the time they reached the studio, the musicians were there too. Freddy said, "It was like a big party. The music, the hand-clapping, the hugs and cheers, the congratulations. Diana was really impressed with what she heard. It was 'Marvin at his very best,' she said."

Marvin's days in Europe were slowly coming to an end. His emotions ran hot and cold, high with creativity and low with knowing that the upcoming release of *Midnight Love,* his new album, meant he would have to return to the United States for promotional appearances. What he didn't know was that Mother was desperately ill, and that he would soon receive a call telling him to rush home.

Perhaps it was the thought of having to leave that prompted "one last look at Belgium." We had driven through the countryside before, months earlier, shortly after my arrival with Irene. My first look took us through one of the country's red-light districts. Marvin had no trouble finding it, and it was truly something to see. Girls in tight, skimpy clothes were walking the streets, standing in doorways, on balconies, and at open windows. Marvin waved, blew kisses, and called out to them as I sank lower in my seat. A good time could easily have been had by all, but we kept going. I couldn't help but wonder where Marvin was taking me this time.

We headed out of Ostend, in the direction of Ohaine, on a road Marvin had traveled many times during the winter, when it was bitterly cold and sometimes impassable because of heavy snowfall. It was late springtime now. The trees were bursting with fresh greenery, and the fields were blazing with bright colors. Aside from not knowing where we were going, I was a little uneasy that we were in a borrowed car and Marvin was without a driver's license. He was feeling adventurous, racing along the road, swerving past cars without looking one way or the other.

We had been gone over an hour when we came to a remote village. Marvin slowed down and pulled off the main road onto a narrow byway that took us past centuries-old houses and through open pasturelands filled with grazing sheep. It was like old times. When we were younger he liked to drive along roads with no addresses. If he'd see an unmarked building, he had to know what was behind the front door. One day he said to me, "Frankie, you go open it. I'll stay in the car." I told him, "There are some things you don't need to know."

Now, as we drove through a grove of trees, he spotted a small church with towering spires. He pulled to a stop. The church looked ancient, with its moss-covered rock walls.

A narrow cobblestone path led us to the heavily carved wooden door. The church was empty, but we went in anyway. Sunlight streamed inside through tall, narrow windows, and a single candle burned up front near the pulpit. Marvin walked on for several yards, his footsteps breaking the silence as he slowly moved along the stone floor. Then I heard another sound. It was Marvin's voice. He was singing, just above a whisper, "The Lord's Prayer." I suddenly felt like we were back in Father's little church in D.C. again; I hadn't heard him sing that way since we were kids. His voice was so clear, so pure, so full of heart.

There were tears in Marvin's eyes when he finished. Mine too, I have to admit. Neither of us spoke for some time after that. In fact, we were in the car on our way back to Ostend before either of us said anything. It was Marvin who spoke first. And then he said only, almost to himself, "It was just me and God."

14

In early October 1982, Marvin boarded a plane for the United States. He had loved being in Belgium, despite the tension that had recently developed between him and Freddy. Marvin credited Freddy for bringing him back from "zombieland," as he put it, but as time went on, and Marvin became clean and healthy again, he began to resent Freddy's control. He also questioned the way Freddy handled the finances. Marvin had to do things his own way.

Marvin was returning to America a big success, yet the ominous feelings that had plagued him prior to his stay in Belgium were beginning to weigh on him again with each airborne mile. Part of it was the long flight, and part of it was the fear that the *Midnight Love* album would be a huge failure. His deepest fear, however, was about Mother. He would have remained in Belgium longer had he not learned that she was critically ill with a kidney infection that required surgery. She was on the operating table as he made his way back home.

Mother, and reaching her in time, filled Marvin's thoughts. He had to be with her, to see her again, to tell her how much he loved her. He had to know she was all right, and that she had pulled through the operation. This operation, any operation, was serious.

The thought of losing her terrified him. She had always been there for him. No way could he not be there for her.

Since Marvin had last set foot in America, he had seemingly turned his life around. His fears about his career, staggering personal debts, lawsuits, even possible jail time, had all been erased. He was thinking straight again. Now this.

Marvin's career was actually on course to hit a new high. He already knew that the single of "Sexual Healing," released a month earlier, had become an immediate hit—the fastest-rising R&B single in the past five years—and it was still climbing the charts. He didn't know it at the time, but his *Midnight Love* album, released only days before his plane took flight, had already reached No. 1, and it would stay at the top of the charts for a then-unprecedented four months. As far as his career was concerned, he had nothing to worry about. Marvin was just being Marvin.

Even as his plane landed in Los Angeles and he stepped onto firm ground again, he could not shake the uncertain feelings that filled his head. Marvin had been virtually drug-free since he had left England. That changed when an entourage of well-wishers and hangers-on were waiting for him in the rented limousine that would take him directly to the hospital.

Mother was still feeling the effects of the anesthesia when Marvin arrived at her bedside. Weak and tired, her body connected to monitoring machines and an IV drip, she was able only to manage a slight smile when she felt Marvin's lips against her cheek. He took her hand and held it in his. "I'm here," he said softly, "I'm here for you." At one point he told her, "If there's anything I can do, Mother, tell me. What can I do?" Mother was silent for a long moment. When she finally started to speak, the words came out so quietly that he couldn't hear her. "Tell me again, Mother. Whatever you want, tell me." He leaned closer to hear her.

It was Mother's wish to call Beatrice Carson, her dearest friend and a cousin by marriage, and get her to come to Los Angeles. Bea had lived with us for years in D.C. when we were kids. She was like a big sister to Mother.

"Marvin called me when his mama was in the hospital and told me what had happened," Bea remembers. "I said I'd come, of course, and started packing. Marvin paid for everything. He sounded so worried."

We were blessed to have Bea with us to help care for Mother. As Bea recalled, "Alberta was so sick, so very sick. I was able to help her during the day, and at night I slept with her in her big king-sized bed, so if she needed anything I was there. When she felt up to it, we talked about old times, anything to cheer her up. I even did most of the cooking, just as I did before they all left to live in Los Angeles. Everyone was so kind to me. They made me feel just like family, which we actually were, in a marriage way."

Another blessing was that just prior to Marvin's arrival home, Father decided to return to D.C. in order to fix up and sell our old house back there. It seemed like an odd time for Father to leave, but in a way, I was glad he did. The friction between Father and Marvin, which had festered over 20 years, was the last thing Mother needed during her convalescence. She was gradually growing stronger but quiet, not conflict, was the best medicine for her at this time.

Father's absence also gave the rest of the family some quality time together. Of course, there was no way we could have known it would be the last chance we would get. When Father returned some weeks later, sister Jeanne moved out. Irene and I were glad to have the house next door all to ourselves. Irene was pregnant with our first child, and she needed as much rest and quiet as possible. We were only a few steps away, but most of the time it felt as if we were miles removed from the tempest brewing next door.

On January 12th, 1983, Marvin found himself at Cedars-Sinai Medical Center in Los Angeles, back in a hospital again, only this time he was all smiles. Irene was about to give birth to our daughter, April. His appearance created quite a commotion, especially among the nurses, who claimed they couldn't concentrate with him around.

Marvin shows off his athletic ability as he pulls in a pass. In 1971 he tried out for the Detroit Lions football team but didn't make the squad. However, football great Jim Brown later said, "Marvin would have been a super jock."

Marvin accepts his Image Award from the NAACP as Producer of the Year for "What's Going On."

When Frankie (left) grew his beard, so did Marvin.

Following a luncheon in his honor at United Nations Headquarters in New York City, Marvin is congratulated for his contribution to the U.S. National Commission for UNESCO by Lemi Lijadu (left), Director of the UNESCO Liaison Office at UN Headquarters. Marvin is flanked by his mother and Shirley Temple Black, U.S. Ambassador to Ghana at the time.

Marvin in London in 1980.

Lady Edith Foxwell with her grandson and, at right, Prince Michael of Kent. During his 1980 England tour, Marvin could often be found at Lady Edith's Wiltshire manor house.

Marvin's mother and father with the family's dog, Angel, in Los Angeles.

Marvin and his mother worshipped each other. They remained close throughout his life.

Onstage at the Greek Theater in Los Angeles during Marvin's final stop on his final tour, in 1983.

Shocked fans gather outside Marvin's house on April 1, 1984, as news of his death is reported. Crowds kept coming as the day went on.

Family and friends gather for a press conference at the Hollywood Roosevelt Hotel to promote a star for Marvin on Hollywood's Walk of Fame. Among those seated at the table are (l-r): Nona Gaye, Jan Gaye, Ron Brewington, and Frankie Gaye. Marvin's star was dedicated on September 27, 1990.

Marvin in concert.

Frankie Gaye.

We had planned a natural childbirth, but once the pains started coming, Irene was begging for anything and everything. "Put me out, please," she cried. She was given an epidural, which made her really thirsty. Soon she was pleading for water, but all a nurse brought her was a tiny cup only partially filled with little ice chips. "No, no," Irene screamed. "I need water, *major* water."

"You can have all the water you want when this is over," the nurse replied.

Irene didn't suffer long. "As the baby was born," she remembers, "a nurse wrapped her in swaddling clothes and took her away to be washed off. Marvin and Frankie disappeared with the nurses. Then my regular nurse came in. 'Now may I have some water, please?' I asked. She looked at me as if I'd gone balmy and said, 'Lady, you'll have to wait. Marvin Gaye's outside.' And with that she was gone. Everybody just left me there."

Irene soon got her water and had a good drink. As soon as she began to relax and fall asleep, Marvin and I went outside, and as we strolled around the hospital grounds, he suddenly said to me, "You know, Frankie, you're the rich one."

"I know," I replied. And I truly believed that.

The next day Irene was able to get out of bed, and I walked with her to the room where the new babies were kept when they weren't with their mothers. As we stood behind the glass looking at little April in her basket, people would come along, stop, and peek at the babies. "That's Marvin Gaye's brother's baby there," one lady gushed, pointing at April.

"It's my baby, too," Irene said quickly.

Irene was so proud of the baby, her first—our first—that she wanted *some* of the credit, at least. After a time, however, she began to take the oversights in stride. "I'd laugh when I'd see heads poke around the door to my room, take a quick look, and leave, whispering, 'That's not her. She's white.' I knew they were really looking for Marvin, and seeing me, their noses went up in the air. They'd looked in the right room but at the wrong time. I never knew if it was April, me, or Marvin, but Cedars-Sinai was buzzing."

Only weeks later, the National Basketball Association invited Marvin to sing the national anthem to open the NBA All-Star Game at the Great Western Forum in Los Angeles. It wasn't the first time Marvin had been asked to sing at an important sports event. In 1968, he opened the World Series when the Detroit Tigers beat the St. Louis Cardinals.

The All-Star Game would be played before a sold-out crowd and televised live to an audience of millions. What excited Marvin most was the chance for him to meet many of the best professional basketball players in the world, stars like Julius Erving, Larry Bird, Moses Malone, Magic Johnson, Kareem Abdul-Jabbar, and Elvin Hayes.

When Marvin told me how he planned to sing the national anthem, with only a drum machine as backing, I told him he was crazy. He replied, "I love the number, and that's the way I hear it."

"But, Marvin, you've got to be more respectful. That song is a national treasure."

He had worked out the concept with his guitarist Gordon Banks, he told me, and he knew it would work. "Besides, I want to do something that's never been done before."

"Then this is it, Marvin. We're packing up the bags and leaving the country for good, because they're going to be looking for you. You can't mess with the national anthem."

"I hear it, man, and that's the way I've got to sing it." Then, typically Marvin, he said, "I won't sing it if I can't sing it my way."

Beneath his confidence and stubbornness, I sensed his uneasiness as the time to sing grew closer. I could almost hear him asking himself if he had what it took to pull off this funky, soulful, sloweddown version of his. Did any singer? He knew if he didn't, this one moment in the spotlight would be a career-killer.

On Sunday, February 13th, Marvin stood courtside at the "Fabulous Forum," hidden by the jumble of press, players, and fans with high-priced tickets. A voice announced, "Now . . . along with the

United States Marine Corps color guard ... to sing the national anthem ... famed recording artist ... Marvin Gaye."

The Forum went wild as Marvin walked to center court wearing a white suit and shades, then the crowd began to hush as the first sounds of the drum machine filled the arena. "Oh, Lord," I prayed, "don't let this go bad."

As Marvin began to sing, I looked around to see the faces in the stands. The people who were eating or talking only moments earlier had put down their hot dogs and popcorn, and were standing still. All eyes were on Marvin; he had everyone's attention. They appeared to be spellbound, totally caught up in what they were hearing.

Midway through, I began to hear scattered hand-clapping to the drum beat as Marvin sang. Then more and more people joined in, until the arena rocked with hand-clapping in unison. It was an incredible moment. I'd heard crowds sing along, but I'd never heard them clap hands *during* the national anthem. The song was too revered for folks to break away from tradition. When I heard cheers and screams of joy as Marvin sang, I told myself to start unpacking. I knew we weren't going to be run out of the country.

The 1983 NBA All-Star Game may be long forgotten after all these years, but Marvin's singing of our anthem has gone down in musical history. Anyone who was at the Forum that day certainly will never forget his performance. Neither will anyone else who heard it worldwide. In the year 2000, as the new century began, the *Los Angeles Times* listed Marvin's version of the national anthem at the All-Star Game among the top-ten performances of the 20th century.

On February 23rd, exactly ten days after the All-Star Game, Marvin was at the Shrine Auditorium in Los Angeles for the 1983 Grammy Awards. He had never won a Grammy, despite earlier nominations for *What's Going On* and *Let's Get It On*. Marvin felt he deserved to win for those albums, but he never did. The winner, both times, was Lou Rawls. Marvin knew that Lou had nothing to do with the vote, but that didn't matter. Just the mention of Lou's name had Marvin fuming. Marvin had lost to Stevie Wonder three times, which never created a ripple. Maybe it was the smile Lou sent Marvin's way after his second win.

Now Marvin was nominated again, but this time he wasn't running against Lou Rawls. It didn't matter; Marvin was nervous anyway. Not only did he have to wait for the winner to be announced, he first had to perform his nominated "Sexual Healing." I was jittery too. From the look in Marvin's eyes I could tell he had spent some time before the show with his cronies.

Marvin somehow got through his performance. It certainly wasn't up to his usual standards, but his fans in the audience joyfully accepted his highs and lows. He was certainly better than he would be during numerous outings over the coming months. (Amazingly, on New Year's Eve, 1999, when the greatest Grammy moments of all time were announced on CBS, Marvin's live performance of "Sexual Healing" from the 1983 show came in ranked at No. 2.)

At last, the nominees for the 1983 Grammys in the R&B categories—Best Male Vocalist and Best Instrumental Performance—were announced, and Marvin came out a double winner. He was thrilled, and the audience was thrilled for him. He didn't even wince when one of his Grammys was presented to him by Jan's latest exboyfriend, Rick James. He simply turned to the crowd, blew a kiss, and said in his soft-spoken way, "Thank you very kindly, ladies and gentlemen, I am not very much for speeches. I'm not much of a public speaker. I always say that. I have waited a very long time, 20-some years to win. Thank you ladies and gentlemen. My family, my friends, my children are out there ... Bubby and Nona, somewhere. Can you stand up, Bubby and Nona, and say hello quickly for us because we can't take a lot of time? We got to go. There they are up there. Love you, baby. My Mom. I love everybody. Thank God. We love you. Stay with us. We're going to try to give you more."

Marvin was truly touched and humbled to win his Grammys. To be honored this late in his career meant even more to him, especially because the awards were given by his peers. "When your peers vote you the best," he said, "that's pretty much the top."

Marvin's great comeback created a new surge of popularity for him, and requests for interviews and guest appearances poured in. Within the next few weeks he appeared on a Dick Clark–produced TV tribute to Gladys Knight and the Pips, on which they sang together for the first time, "I Heard It Through the Grapevine." He joined Motown's 25th anniversary special, which reunited many former Motown artists. Taped at the Pasadena Civic Auditorium on March 25th, 1983, "Motown 25: Yesterday, Today, Forever" was spectacular entertainment, a flashback to the Motortown Revues of old, with one popular act after another performing hit upon hit, in rapid succession. It was truly a celebration of "the sound that rocked the world."

Marvin sang "What's Going On," the hit that gave him creative independence at Motown, and he began it as if he were back at Hitsville, when Berry Gordy first took notice of him at the company Christmas party. Sitting at a piano onstage, he gently let his fingers roam the keys, coolly improvising soft, melancholy chords that led him into the opening bars of the specially written verse. It was an emotional performance that some reporters labeled as drug-induced.

For the finale, each of the Motown artists returned to the stage, where they joined Diana Ross in a sing-along of "Some Day We'll Be Together," taking a moment to hug and kiss Berry Gordy. Even Marvin managed to give his former boss a squeeze.

When "Motown 25" was televised nationally seven weeks later, Marvin was touring the country. Not everyone involved liked the fact that the show had been heavily edited, but it still attracted the biggest audience in American television history to date, and won an Emmy for the season's Most Outstanding Variety Program.

Marvin had come home to America from Europe to finally be recognized by his peers, and to be received lovingly by audiences wherever he appeared. But he was about to take to the road again, this time to begin his next, and last, national tour, one that would have him fighting for his life.

15

*M*arvin wasn't anxious to go on the road again, but as always, money was the prodding force. As much as he wanted to avoid the pressures of live performing, he knew he had no choice. And once Marvin made up his mind to do something, nothing, or no one, could stop him.

His first American tour in nearly four years, and his most extensive in nearly ten years, had to top everything he had ever done, not only in the number of tour stops but in production values. Concerts were targeted for cities across America over a four-month period, starting in San Diego in mid-April and ending in Los Angeles in mid-August. Everything had to be new, Marvin said, and looking great. Specifically, he meant the costumes, his backup singers and dancers, and even himself.

"Marvin went through periods of eating right and counting calories," remembers Dave Simmons, his good friend from the Detroit days. A former high school basketball coach and director of a youth program, Dave and Marvin hit it off from the start. Along with sports stars Dave Bing, Lem Barney, and Bob Lanier, he became one of Marvin's running partners. They hung out in gyms together, played hoops, and playfully beat up on each other. When Marvin moved to California, Dave Simmons followed a year later. Many mornings would find them running along the beach in Santa Monica. Dave says, "Marvin liked looking good, so he was always on some sort of trick diet to get me and Frankie on. He had us eating nothing but nasty vegetables, then we'd catch him eating a cheeseburger around the corner."

Shortly after finishing the "Motown 25" TV special, Marvin and his valet, Odell George ("Gorgeous George"), left for Palm Springs to get Marvin into shape for his upcoming tour. He had "basically sworn off drugs," he said, and was back into vitamins in a big way. He had put out calls to Gloria Carlyle, his vitamin guru, who at one time ran rejuvenation clinics in Mexico. Marvin hadn't seen Gloria since he'd returned from Europe. After working so hard with Freddy Cousaert to get clean in Belgium, he had started sliding again. Now it was important for him to get back in touch with Gloria.

It was Kitty Sears, a frontwoman for many of the Motown artists, who first introduced Gloria Carlyle to Marvin. At the time, around 1977 as Gloria remembers, she knew of Marvin but she wasn't interested in working with him—but he refused to take no for an answer. "Kitty nagged me to death," says Gloria, "until I finally agreed to let her take me to his recording studio on Sunset Boulevard. From the moment I met Marvin I was really impressed, not only with his sensitivity and creativity, but with his brilliance. He was so well-read and knew so much about so many diverse things. He was amazing. He knew about GH3, the youth vitamins that came from Romania, which all the stars were into at the time. Even though it wasn't legal in the United States, he wanted his arteries to be as clear as they possibly could be. There has been so much emphasis on Marvin's cocaine use, and all of that, but he was really quite interested in good health and in improving his physical condition."

Gloria, Kitty, and Marvin wound up talking until five in the morning. As the two ladies were finally about to leave, Gloria admired a huge framed picture of Marvin on one of the studio walls. It had been taken only months earlier while he was performing at the Palladium in London. "It was a fantastic shot," says Gloria, "a massive thing. Some photographer had captured him at just the perfect split-second. I guess he could tell how much the photo impressed me, because he suddenly reached up and, heavy as it was, lifted it off the wall. 'Here, it's yours,' he said. I backed off, saying, 'No, no, it belongs in your studio.' Marvin looked disappointed as he set the huge frame down. But the next day he had his man, Odell George, bring me a pair of diamond stud earrings. He was very spontaneous, very generous."

From that point on, Marvin and Gloria were good friends. It was an odd friendship, which in time grew even stronger, despite Gloria's stand on drugs, cigarettes, alcohol, and all things harmful to the body; she didn't even drink coffee. And while they hadn't seen one another since his return to California, she had remained in Marvin's thoughts. He had great respect for Gloria, and he admired her strength. It was also hard to forget her good looks: she was tall, blonde, and glamorous.

Now, as Marvin readied for his extended tour of America, he and Gloria found themselves together in Palm Springs. She had come to the desert with a girlfriend, an accountant, and Marvin was there with George. One night they all met for dinner. "Marvin was very cleaned up," Gloria remembers. "He was taking intramuscular shots of GH3, which I had obtained from my former husband, a doctor in Beverly Hills who had suffered from rheumatoid arthritis. The ampules of GH3 came from one of his patients who had been on a movie shoot in Europe. Anyway, Marvin was in tip-top shape with his shots, massages, his working out, and watching what he ate.

"The hotel was very crowded ... all around the pool, the lobby, everyplace. But I didn't see one African American. I thought, 'Oh, my God, poor Marvin and George.' I felt awkward for them. Walking along, however, an older woman stopped him to talk, and almost immediately, everyone began responding to him. He was so gracious, kind, and compassionate, and he showed such a real interest in people. He would say to each person as he went on his way, 'And God bless you,' with such sincerity. You could tell he wasn't just tossing off the words, he truly meant them. He had everyone in his pocket as we made our way to the dining room.

"My only problem with Marvin that evening was the way he introduced me to the people we met, strangers and friends alike. Instead of just giving my name, he'd say, 'And this is my love.' I certainly got some very strange looks."

Marvin was in excellent shape on April 18th as he opened his tour in San Diego. He looked wonderful, and everyone in the arena was anticipating a sensational show, wildly yelling and stomping even before the announcer's words blasted through the amped-up loud-speakers.

"Creator of funk, author of soul, one of the classic, most creative, most publicized entertainers in the world . . . two-time Grammy winner . . . entertainer of the year . . . American Music Award winner . . . Columbia recording star, Mr. Marvin Gaye!!!"

Wearing a long white coat that flared out as he raised his arms to acknowledge the ear-splitting reception from the crowd, Marvin walked out onstage. He was beaming, seemingly overwhelmed, yet confident, and thrilled to be back in the spotlight.

The expensive two-and-a-half-hour show ran long, but few people minded. Marvin was back, the show was great, and so were his fans. Gloria, too, was impressed, and not only because he had dedicated a song to her. "It was exciting," she said, "and afterward Marvin had somebody take me backstage. Mike Love of the Beach Boys was there, and I met Frankie, Irene, and their baby, April, for the first time. He put April in my arms to see how I'd look with a baby and I said, 'Forget it.' He wanted me to drive back to Los Angeles with him but I refused. I didn't want to be with some of the oddballs in his entourage."

In San Diego, Marvin sang like a million dollars, even though he had opening-night jitters; they weren't noticeable. Inside, he told me, he was a wreck. His morbid fear of performing before audiences had him nearly paralyzed with fear. The fact is, Marvin never should have left home. San Diego was only the first of many more such nights ahead. There would be audiences from coast to coast, border to border, and it would be downhill from this point on. Although Marvin felt he knew how to take some of the edge off his fear, and he made no secret about it, his fears would only increase. Drugs were not his friend. It's been said that the devil was on this tour.

Despite a deepening depression, Marvin remained "the grand admiral of soul." He even wore an awesome designer's version of high-military gear, complete with gold braid, buttons, and epaulets on his shoulders—and this was pre–Michael Jackson—to sock home his lofty ranking. Coming across as cool and cocksure, he thrilled audiences in sold-out venues with his pure vocal skills and sexy moves. But his voice was beginning to take on a rough edge, and his suggestions of sex were becoming less subtle, more blatant. When I saw him unbutton his shirt onstage, then take it off, I wondered how many push-ups it took to get him to do that. As the tour wore on, he became even more revealing, turning his concerts into musical sex shows. His onstage comments took on a different tone too, when he began to tell his fans that he feared there was little time left for mankind. "The gloom is real," he'd say, "and doom is our fate. Five more years, ten at the most, then it will be over." As it turned out, he had much less time than that.

Strange things were happening backstage, as well. Cohorts were filling Marvin's head with ugly thoughts, which he turned into his personal problems. There were complaints from African Americans, he was told, that he wasn't using enough black drivers, caterers, helpers. He learned that a member of his road crew, Eric Sharpe, had threatened suicide, then went through with it by hanging himself from a shower curtain rod. And on top of all that, Marvin was increasingly obsessed with conspiracy theories.

In Indianapolis, unknown to Marvin or to any of his key people, a recording was made of his performance and released *17 years later* as *Marvin Gaye: The Final Concert*. It wasn't the final concert, since many more stops were still to be played, but it was part of the final tour. Too bad better equipment wasn't used to record the event. In fact, it's obvious that professional equipment wasn't used at all and that nothing had been set up onstage. More likely, a fan had taped the concert on a portable cassette recorder, which is probably the reason it took so long to be released. Had it been recorded properly it surely would have been a runaway bestseller after Marvin's death in April 1984.

The poor quality aside, Marvin's performance in Indianapolis wasn't even one of his best during the final tour, and certainly not the one to be preserved forever for his fans. It was a night to remember, however, especially for the backstage confusion and chaotic atmosphere in Marvin's dressing room. Marvin was sky-high, and not with eagerness to get onstage. I begged him not to go on in his condition, or at least to delay the start of the concert until he came down some. But, as usual, he wouldn't listen. He insisted he could go on, and he did.

Unless Marvin was totally drugged-out, he could sing; not always great, but pretty good. That's because he was so familiar with his material. It was what he did between songs that had his audiences either shaking their heads, bewildered, or smiling knowingly and egging him on. His patter was so often filled with pauses and unfocused thoughts that it was obvious he didn't know where he was headed. He simply rambled. But night after night he got through it. And if he got stuck, he'd start singing. That's what his fans came to hear anyway, he figured.

"Marvin called me from New York," says Gloria Carlyle. "He was about to start his engagement at Radio City Music Hall and he wanted to show me his favorite city, 'his New York,' as he called it. 'I love the people, I love the energy, I love the diversity,' he said. Then he added, 'I want you to come right away, please.' I told him I couldn't, I didn't have time. I explained that business involvements had me traveling. 'Please come,' he repeated. Finally I told him I just couldn't, and ended it with 'I'm not a groupie!'"

According to Gloria, Marvin kept calling and calling, and she kept turning him down. Then she began receiving messages from Kitty Sears. When they finally hooked up, Kitty said, "It's terrible what's happening to Marvin."

"What's happening?" Gloria asked.

"You should be here for him," she said. "He needs you."

Gloria responded, "Marvin always used to tell me that he needed my strength, and I'd tell him, 'Develop some of your own. Knock this off.'" Gloria was always up-front with Marvin, totally outspoken and honest. He liked that about her. She was one of the few people who wasn't a bobbing head in his presence.

It was easy for Marvin to open up to Gloria. He once told her, "You know, in the past I could lock myself up in a room for six weeks, have food shipped in, and I could get cleaned up and brand new." But that was then. The older he got, the more swamped he became with his trials and tribulations, and the more possessed by drugs he became, the harder it was for him to turn things around. "And being completely surrounded by drugs," says Gloria, "it became overwhelming for him."

Marvin's phone calls, followed by Kitty's urgent calls, had Gloria packing. "I hopped on a plane with more vitamins, some new DHEA, and other nutritional supplements he probably wasn't familiar with. I didn't want to stay at the Waldorf, where Marvin was staying, because I wanted to avoid his entourage. So I registered across the street. Kitty met me with word that Marvin was really in bad shape." Her other news was that Jan was in town with Rick James, and that lots of drugs were going down. "I don't want to see Marvin like that," she told Kitty.

Then George called her. "Marvin will kick somebody out and give you a front-row seat," he told her. How Marvin could have arranged that, I don't know. The Radio City Music Hall engagement was sold *solid* for all eight performances.

After what Kitty had told Gloria, she was noncommittal. "I don't know," she replied. "Let me think about it."

Not a minute passed before Gloria's hotel-room phone rang again. It was Marvin. Gloria remembers, "He was still in some ways kind of shy. He was so afraid of rejection, surprisingly, that he would have someone call first to see how you were feeling or the kind of mood you were in. He had to have someone else test the waters, so to speak, to break the ice. When he asked me to come to his hotel, I said frankly, 'Marvin, I can't get involved in any of this. The only reason I'm here is because you called me so often and offered to show me New York.' He went silent for a long moment before he replied that he didn't remember. 'You what?' I snapped. 'I break my neck, almost kill myself to get to New York, and you don't remember telling me how this is your town, and all that?' He said only, 'Well, not really.' With that I begged off seeing him and his show, and I returned to Los Angeles."

In Baltimore, Dick Gregory happened to be staying in our hotel while we were in town, and he visited Marvin. "Dick came to Marvin's room and talked to him about his drug use," says Dave Simmons. "When Dick heard we had four days off before the next concert, he generously opened his home in Massachusetts to Marvin. 'You can stay there and be quiet,' Dick told him. 'Take it easy and have a nice, relaxing stay, and get yourself together.'" The political activist, who was also heavily into nutrition and colonics for better health, waited patiently for Marvin to respond to his offer. When Marvin's answer came, it was simply, "Aw, okay." Then he fell asleep.

Dave continues: "When Marvin woke up he asked me where everybody went. I told him they all took off during the break in the schedule, which he already knew. He looked at me and said, 'What! Oh, my goodness. What do you mean they're gone?' I told him, 'It's just you and me. We're it.' I reminded Marvin about Dick Gregory's offer and started to pack his clothes and everything into a garment bag. We were set to leave, or so I thought, when Marvin said he couldn't do it. 'Go upstairs and tell Dick I've changed my mind. Tell him I'm sorry... and tell him I'll give ten thousand dollars to any charity he names.'

"So I went upstairs to Dick Gregory's room, told him Marvin wouldn't go, and he went off on me. 'What do you mean he's not interested?' he shouted. 'Oh, he's interested but he just said he can't go,' I replied. 'Now he can't go, huh?' said Dick, starting to pace furiously. 'Do you know what I've done? I called and had some people moved out of the house so we'd have room for him. I'm supposed to be in Helsinki and I postponed that. I gotta call my wife!' Dick stopped pacing and jumped on the phone. I heard him say, 'He's not coming so go ahead and make arrangements for the flight to Helsinki.'" At that point I thought I'd better tell Dick about Marvin's offer of a donation to his choice of charities. That certainly helped smooth things over, because his whole attitude immediately changed. But his earlier visit with Marvin was the last time they'd talk to each other."

Things got so bad in New Haven that Dave Simmons and I tried to get Marvin to cancel the rest of the tour and let us take him home. It wasn't easy to get close to Marvin because he had so many crazy goons hanging around him all the time. But it got to the point where we had to tell him it was time to stop. It was close to show-time when we cornered him in his dressing room. He certainly was in no condition to go onstage. "Man, I can't... I can't afford... I don't know...."

"Well, it was your mother's suggestion that we get you back home," said Dave, using the magic word.

"Oh, wow, Mother said that?"

"She sure did," Dave replied.

"Aw, man, she knows about things like this. Well... okay."

That did it—or so we thought. Next thing we knew, Marvin was refusing to leave. His hangers-on had gotten to him and convinced him that Dave was putting out bad vibes. "They were always trying to get rid of me and Frankie," Dave remembers. "We'd tell

Marvin, 'Those fools are crazy, man, they're nuts. All they want to do is keep you high as much as possible.'"

As long as Marvin was working they knew they had it good. They were messing with his mind, whispering in his head, constantly. Every day it was something different, and the next day was more hectic than the last.

As the tour continued, Marvin believed someone was out to kill him. He couldn't sleep, and he picked at his food, because a seed had been planted that he might be poisoned. For any fan of classic movies, it was like watching Ingrid Bergman squirm as Charles Boyer slowly tried to drive her insane in *Gaslight*. But that was only a movie, and this was real. It was also my brother who was possibly being stalked. Suffering from exhaustion, dehydration, and a suspected lung infection, Marvin collapsed in Florida and was rushed to a hospital. Seven days later, weak and still ill, he returned to the stage.

"Marvin called me from Florida," says Gloria. "He told me he had bought a condo or something down there and he wanted me to see this, that, and the other. But after being burned with the New York thing, I didn't know what to believe. He didn't mention anything about his sickness."

Back on the road, Marvin began receiving threatening phone calls and notes—or so he said. I began to wonder if they were real or imagined. If the threats were real, were they made by people who were actually out to get Marvin or by those who wanted to make him nervous, just to remain on his payroll?

It seemed everyone who worked for Marvin was now carrying guns. Marvin became so paranoid that he wanted me and Dave Simmons to be his bodyguards. We went everywhere with him. He even had us check out each hotel in every city before he'd step inside. It was the same thing coming back to our hotel after a concert. "We'd leave the arena in whatever city we were in," says Dave, "and he'd have us circle the hotel three or four times to see if anyone was tailing us. Then Frankie and I would look at each other and shake our heads."

Getting off elevators on the way to our rooms was an adventure, too. If we were staying on the fifth floor, we had to punch seven to trick whoever might be following us. It never made me or Dave feel any safer, because we both were head-to-toe ringers for Marvin: same height, same build, same look. We were like triplets wherever we went. If Marvin was a marked man, so were we.

One late night, as our elevator doors opened onto the phony floor, we pushed Dave out. "I'm standing out in the hall," he remembers, "and the elevator doors closed behind me. They'd gone on to wherever they were going and I'm thinking, 'Dang, man, what if Marvin's right? We'd been telling him all along "There's nobody," but what if we were wrong?'"

I felt the same way whenever I had to exit first, especially when the elevator doors opened onto our actual floor. Nothing ever happened, but those first few steps into the unknown were always scary.

Standing slightly off to the side during Marvin's performances wasn't much fun either. We were all easy targets; anyone in the audience could have had us in his (or her) sights. It was frightening every time Marvin went onstage, having to face all those people in the audience, wonderful and loving fans all, but it would have taken only one who wasn't to mess things up. There were so many times when I wondered if bullets were to fly, who would get hit—Marvin, Dave, or me? What about the dancers, singers, and musicians? When I mentioned that to Marvin, he simply smiled. That wasn't reassuring, but down deep, I couldn't help but feel that the dangers were imagined. Marvin's problem was in his head. My job was more to reassure him than to protect him. Marvin probably knew that too, because he kept saying, "God protects me."

Through it all, Marvin somehow kept on going. By August, as the tour was winding down, he talked of Europe again, and of a new, different, sexier tour, with a side trip to Finland, and possibly New

Zealand. That was not to be. He was too exhausted, too weak, too possessed. There were times when he tried to swear off drugs, but they were all around him, wherever he went. His resistance was low, and the temptation was too overpowering.

Marvin had to get away. He had to escape his real-life demons, and the demons in his head. Ending the travel-weary tour, he believed, was his only hope. Now that time had arrived as he headed home to Los Angeles for what would turn out to be his final concerts. Waiting for him there were the only two women he claimed he ever trusted: Mother and Gloria.

16

Back in Los Angeles after four months on the road, Marvin checked into L'Ermitage, one of Beverly Hills's most exclusive hotels. "I thought we were going to the house," I said.

"You are," he replied. "I'm staying here."

"What about Mother?"

"I'm calling her first thing," he said. "Got to talk with her. Got to let her know I'm back in town."

That sounded more like Marvin. He was so good about calling Mother from the road. I doubt if he missed a day, no matter how he felt or what was going on. But another hotel? He had to be sick of them by now. His excuse was that he'd be closer to the Greek Theater, where he was closing down his tour with a series of shows starting the following night. In terms of miles, Beverly Hills probably wasn't any closer to the Greek Theater than the house on Gramercy Place. I was sure he had something else going on. He hadn't snorted coke for at least 24 hours; I knew that because I'd been with him every second of that time. But I didn't question him. I couldn't wait to see Irene and April, sleep in my own house again, and eat some of Irene's good home cooking.

It wasn't until later that I learned why Marvin wasn't rushing to get home. He had more than one phone call to make after I left him. He had to talk with Gloria too.

"Marvin called me as soon as he got into Los Angeles," Gloria said. "He was staying at L'Ermitage and he wanted me to come to dinner. I was happy to hear from him so I said okay. He sounded good.

"When I got to the hotel there were several men with Marvin in his suite, part of his entourage, I guess. I'm sure he wasn't on anything at all at the time because he seemed to be in great shape. We ate in his suite, served by two of his men, who kind of disappeared once we'd finished. He had so much to tell me, he said, stories about his tour, even some of the bad things that had happened. One thing I found so fascinating about Marvin was that he was so totally honest, almost like a child. Then he started talking about his upcoming shows at the Greek. He was going to come out in his shorts or do something shocking and sexy, he told me, but out of respect for me he said he wouldn't. 'There's a song I want to dedicate to you, but if that will embarrass you, I won't do that either.' He knew I'd be there because tickets were coming from either Kitty or George.

"I thanked him for being so sensitive to my feelings, then told him I really didn't go for that sexy business onstage. I thought it was demeaning to him, changed his whole image, and made a mockery of his talent. 'You know,' he said, 'it was never my idea to begin with. Berry Gordy wanted me to be a singing sex god. I never wanted that, but once I saw that the ladies liked it, I kept it in. Sex was never my focus but it worked. Then I had to keep trying to top myself.' He was about to say more when there was a tapping on the door to his suite. He looked around for his guys but they weren't around. Marvin excused himself and went to the door. I heard a lot of whispering.

"Not too far from the front door," Gloria says, "was a bathroom. I heard the door to the suite close as the whispering continued, then another door closed. I figured Marvin and his visitor—or visitors—

had gone into the bathroom to talk. In a flash, I thought, 'Gloria, you can't get involved in anything like this.' I knew it was drugs, it had to be. I got up and left."

As Gloria remembers, her phone rang all night long. She didn't pick up the receiver until the next morning. It was Kitty. "How could you do this to Marvin?" she wanted to know. "He's destroyed. He's not going to perform tonight. You left him when he had only high hopes."

"I'm sorry," Gloria told her. "I know it was drugs and I won't, and I can't, and that's it."

Marvin did show up at the Greek Theater that night to do his show, and Gloria was there. "It was a total disaster," she says. "The music was so loud you could hardly hear him, but it didn't make any difference. He was so drugged-up, so bad. When he told me at dinner he had tickets for me we made plans to meet after the show, but I didn't even go backstage."

Marvin went into a deep, deep depression, thinking he had lost Gloria and his dreams for the future. He worshipped Gloria, even though their time together had been limited. He fantasized about her, wanted desperately to marry her, had proposed to her twice and would again. He had tried to be at his best when they were together. She knew about his failings; he had always tried to be honest with her. He knew she truly cared for him and wanted to help him. But now she was gone and ugly thoughts filled his mind. He feared he would never see her again.

By the time Marvin made his way back to Mother's side, his de-mons were working overtime. It was hard to figure Marvin out, al-most impossible to know how to react to him. One minute he could be his fine self, or almost himself, and be over-the-top the next. When he was high his thoughts were only of bad things. He talked of death much too much. There was no escaping death, he would say. He knew it was coming, and soon.

Marvin truly believed that he had come home to die. He men-tioned suicide, but there would be no suicide for Marvin, even though he had threatened to take his own life in Hawaii. We had talked about the act of suicide as kids when we were Bible readers under Father's thumb. We had learned then that it was wrong, and Marvin's beliefs were still too strong. He wanted peace in his new life. "I could never ask forgiveness," he had said.

Home had always been Marvin's safe haven, no matter what had been happening in his life. But home was not a happy place for Marvin on his return. Mother was still recuperating from her surgery; it was difficult enough for her to care for herself, let alone Marvin. But Mother was too giving and loving. It was impossible for her to let Marvin down. Bea had returned to her family in D.C. Now Mother basically had to tend to the house on her own. When things got really rough she would call Irene or me to come over from next door.

Father seemed never to be in a good mood. He was upset that Marvin had moved back in. They sniped at each other a lot, and their arguments became fierce at times. It became quiet only when one or the other, or both of them, stayed in their separate bedrooms.

There were days when I spent more time in the main house than I spent in mine, with Irene and April. Marvin had grown suspicious of anyone who came to the door, friends and strangers alike. He wouldn't leave the house, and there were times when he begged me not to leave, even if only to get the mail or a newspaper. "Aren't you afraid to go outside?" he would ask.

Some days were better than others. Dave Simmons liked to spend time with Marvin whenever he could. Often they would sit together in Marvin's room while Marvin read his Bible. One time, as Dave remembers, "I found Marvin walking around in his bathrobe, no clothes, just his bathrobe." Another time Father pulled Dave aside. "He told me Marvin had been beating him. When Marvin stopped, he told his father he was leaving but he'd be back to have at him again." Dave didn't know what to make of that because he knew we'd been taught not to hit anyone, especially our parents. Later, to try to ease the tension between Marvin and Father, Dave told Father how Marvin had dedicated a song from his *Midnight Love* album to him during each show on the last tour. It was the song "Joy," with its beat like Pentecostal church music. Dave says, "He beamed when I told him how Marvin had praised him and his preaching, and had told the crowd that the song was played in his church. "He looked at me and said, 'Aw, Dave, you're just saying that.' I replied, 'No, sir, it's true. It really is,' and all he could say was, 'Oh, man.'" Deep down he loved Marvin dearly, but he was a proud, intelligent man. He had such strong beliefs, and Marvin's footing all the bills created a bad situation.

Gloria too had words for Father. She was back in Marvin's life again after one phone call. "Marvin had sort of disappeared after he went back home. Then one day he called and said, 'I'm at my Mother's and I'm turning over a new leaf.' He wanted me to get him various vitamins and he asked me to come over. He'd written a new song he wanted me to hear. I said okay.

"Marvin was almost courtly in his manners and graciousness. No matter who it was or where we went, if he saw a man washing windows or whatever, he would go over and talk to him like a long-lost friend. He had a wonderful kindness and sweetness about him. I commended him for being so unpretentious and he replied, 'You know, I have my Father to thank for that. He taught me discipline, which I could use more of, as well as manners and how to conduct myself as a gentleman.' I repeated what Marvin had told me to his father, who straightened proudly, and with a smile, he said, 'Did he really? I'm pleased to hear that.'"

During Gloria's first visit to the house she had a chance to meet Mother. "She was a wonderful woman," says Gloria, "one of the wisest, kindest women in the world. She told me how she cooked for Marvin every day, sat on the edge of his bed, and literally forced him to eat. With the drugs he wouldn't want to eat, but she made him."

According to Gloria, Marvin seemed to be doing fine whenever she saw him. He told her he had made plans to sing again, and he wanted her to hear his new song. "I sat down next to him as he started playing a beautiful melody on the piano," she remembers. "All of a sudden, from all around came tap … tap … tap on the windows.

Marvin got up and went somewhere as a young lady, a niece, I believe, opened the door. Three men stood there; two of them were
way over six feet tall. They were massive, like bodyguards. They came
inside, looked at me, and sat down on the sofa. 'Where's Marvin?' the
smallest man asked. The niece was gone, leaving only me to answer.
'He's upstairs, busy for a moment,' I alibied. 'Well, we've come to get
him.' I backed away a bit and said, 'Get him for what?' The man explained that Marvin was supposed to appear at Marla Gibbs's Memory Lane Jazz Supper Club. 'The place is packed,' he said, 'and people
are out in the street, waiting to get in. We've come to get him ... take
him to the club. He's late.'"

By this time, as Gloria remembers, it was not only getting late,
but according to one of the men, Marvin was supposed to have been
at the club over an hour ago. Marvin had a reputation for not showing up for performances, but this time, according to Gloria, he had
actually forgotten.

Gloria remembers trying to calm the men down by telling them
that Marvin had not been well, and that tonight he had come down
with food poisoning or something. "I made up some lies, which
seemed to work, so when Marvin came downstairs the men's stares
weren't quite so threatening."

Gloria offered to go with Marvin to Marla Gibbs's place. "He
didn't think that was such a good idea, I guess, because he replied,
'Wouldn't you feel uneasy being the only white face in the crowd?'
I told him, 'Not really. I've been everywhere in the world and have
been the only one. It's never bothered me. People are people.'"

Gloria did admit, however, that she felt uneasy when Marvin
labeled the three men who came for him as members of the Black
Mafia. Even Marvin admitted to being scared. She said he told her
that he was on thin ice with them, and praised her for standing up
for him.

During another of Gloria's visits to the house, Marvin took
Gloria's keys and hid them because he didn't want her to leave. That
same evening, she heard more tapping on the windows. "Nephews

and everybody were bringing him drugs and wanting money," she said. "I went to the door with Marvin standing not far behind me, and some kids were there. 'I have something for Marvin,' one of them said, and I asked, 'What?' The kid looked back at Marvin, then at me. 'Something to help him sleep,' the youngster replied in a cocky way. He held out a packet of something, expecting Marvin to step forward. I pushed the kid's hand away and said, 'Get out of here, all of you. Marvin can have some hot milk.' They must have thought I was nuts, but Marvin laughed and the kids left.

"There was always someone tapping on the windows," Gloria recalls. "Even if Marvin was trying to get clean, or so he'd tell me, there was always someone pushing drugs in his face. It never stopped. I tried to get Marvin to take his knowledge of drugs into the neighborhood and talk to the kids. 'You can talk to anyone,' I told him. 'They'll listen to you.' But he wouldn't do it."

Gloria went through some crazy times with Marvin, sad times too, but good or bad, she kept responding to his calls. One thing that especially endeared him to her, no matter his condition, was that he was always so proper when they were together. "I'd say things like 'darn' and 'damn' and he'd say, 'Gloria, that isn't nice to talk that way,' and I'd come back with, 'Well, excuse me all to heck.' I didn't use a lot of profanity, but I did say stupid things like, 'How are you, you little dumpling?' and he loved that. If I'd get upset with him and say, 'Darn your stupid hide,' he'd reply, 'I guess I'm not your little dumpling today.' If I was really upset, I'd add, 'No, you aren't any sort of dumpling, blast it, so shape up.'"

As the weeks passed, Marvin and Gloria saw a lot of each other. One day after Gloria had been to the house, Marvin asked Mother, "What do you think of me marrying Gloria?"

"Well," she replied, "you've been married to two black women. Why not try a white woman?" Mother was half-joking, Marvin said, but in a kind, thoughtful way.

Marvin proposed to Gloria for the third time and, with the help of "Soul Train" host, Don Cornelius, began looking for his dream house in Bel Air. He specifically wanted a place with one enormous room so he could cover the walls with books. He wanted only to read "every book under the sun" and write music, never to perform again. But Gloria turned Marvin down, and he went into another tailspin.

From my window across the way, I could see people approaching the house and tapping on the windows. It was impossible for anyone to see inside because the shades were always pulled down. Marvin wanted it that way. He liked it dark and gloomy. From time to time, he would wander about cautiously in his robe, carrying his Bible in his hands and a gun in his pocket. He was heavily into drugs again. His demons had returned and his paranoia was as intense as when we were on the road. He was certain he was a marked man.

Seeing Marvin this way frightened me, and each day I grew more and more frightened. One minute he talked about being with angels, then he talked about not being loved. When I told him that millions of people loved him, he replied, "Nobody really loves me. There's nobody I can trust anymore." There was no reasoning with Marvin; it was impossible to reach him. He was breaking my heart.

Around Christmas 1983, Gloria excitedly called Irene and me from San Francisco, where she was setting up a TV show. She called to tell us that Marvin needed professional help very badly, but the good news was that she had been in touch with a Scottish woman who had developed a revolutionary new treatment for drug addicts. It had proven successful with many prominent people, including rock stars. "I traced her through one of the medical journals," said Gloria, "and found her on vacation in Hawaii. She has a clinic on an island off the coast near Seattle. She said she'd cut short her time in Hawaii and set everything up to help Marvin. This is a state-of-the-art treatment, without any withdrawal or sense of loss or turmoil. But, Frankie, in order to get Marvin to agree to go up there, we need you to go with him. Will you go?"

"Yes," I said, "I will."

"And Irene," Gloria went on, "will you get Marvin ready, please? I've spent days putting this together and I want it to work."

"Oh, yes," Irene said.

Gloria then asked me to go over to the main house. She was going to call Marvin within the next few minutes and wanted me to be with him.

When the phone rang in the main house, Marvin didn't want to answer it, but I told him it was Gloria calling. At the sound of her voice he perked up immediately and listened to what she had to say. Then I heard him say, "All right, come and get me."

Gloria explained that she couldn't because she was in San Francisco, but I would go with him. She told him if he didn't want to take a cab to the airport, she would arrange for a limo. The tickets would be at the airline counter and he would be met at the airport in Seattle. Everything had been set up for two days later.

Gloria emphasized to Marvin that he would be in the best hands. These are the greatest people, the greatest scientists, she assured him, and this could be the beginning of a new life for him. Then she added, "You've got to make an extreme change, Marvin. This is what you've wanted."

"Well, all right," he said. "Let me talk to Frankie."

Gloria repeated that I was going with him, and that he wouldn't be alone.

Over the next day and a half, Gloria was on the phone to Marvin, Irene, and me, to make sure we were all together. On the day we were set to leave, she called again. "Marvin, are you ready?" she asked.

Marvin said he couldn't go.

Gloria let him have it. "How dare you!" she said. "These people are waiting for you. They've canceled everything for you, put everything on the line for you, and you just want to wallow in what you're doing to yourself. Get yourself together!"

"Well, you won't come after me," he replied.

"Don't you understand, Marvin, I can't. Right now I've got eight people depending on me for a live TV show. I'm not even in Los Angeles."

"I'm afraid," Marvin said.

"Afraid of what?"

"Of being locked up."

"You're not going to be locked up," Gloria said. "They do not lock you up. You'll be in cottages on an island off the coast, being taken care of by the most qualified people. These are wonderful scientists with credentials up the wazoo."

Marvin mumbled and carried on. Gloria said only, "I'm furious, Marvin," and hung up. A few minutes later, she called him back. "Okay, Marvin, this is the end of the line. I'm not going to play any more games. I've said everything there is to say. Either you want to get well or you don't. The choice is yours."

"Come for me," Marvin said.

"I cannot!"

"I'm afraid."

"Goodbye, Marvin," Gloria said. She hung up the phone and never talked to him again.

As the days passed, Marvin called her, Kitty called her, George called her, but Gloria held her ground. "I went so far," she told me, "and I couldn't do any more. He was a wonderful guy. He had a sense of humanity and kindness. I loved him as a person, and as a man, but…"

Along the way, so many people had tried to help Marvin, but after continually being turned down they cut themselves off. It was too difficult watching him destroy himself.

From here on it was all downhill for Marvin. It got to the point where Mother couldn't stand being in the main house. Father had become really jealous of the attention Mother gave to Marvin, and he was getting on her nerves. She decided to come next door and spend a night with Irene, April, and me, but she wound up staying longer.

Irene remembers those days. "Mother Gay wasn't feeling very well, so I cooked for all of us. I even made extra. She'd ask me to take a plate over to Marvin, which infuriated Father Gay. One time after I'd taken a plate to Marvin, Father Gay called Frankie to say, 'Do you know your wife is in Marvin's bedroom?' He was always trying to stir things up."

Father had to keep an eye on what we were doing next door, too. There were times when Mother and I would go to the store and we could see him peeking out of his window as we drove off. At the store we'd buy Marvin his favorite things to tempt him to eat; he especially liked Häagen-Dazs ice cream. When we came home, we'd see Father still watching as we carried in the bags of food. Then he'd call Mother and ask when she was coming back, and why we never bought anything for him. He had become the forgotten man because Mother didn't want to deal with him anymore. He was so verbally abusive to her. He never hit her, but he raised his voice and said really hurtful things.

Father loved attention. He especially liked it when people complimented him on his "pretty legs," which is why he always wore shorts, white shorts, cut high. Father had seen the way the ladies swarmed around Marvin, but paid him no attention. That, along with Marvin's success singing "the wrong kind of music," built up a lot of anger and jealousy over the years.

It has been wrongly reported that Father cheated on Mother when he was younger. The fact is, along with being a minister, he was a counselor as well, and people would come to the house with their problems. In those days, when we lived in D.C., I'd see him take people, mostly women, up to his room and close the door. There was never a hint of scandal then, but once I did hear Mother ask him, "Why do you always have to shut the door?"

And the rumor that Father wore women's clothes? Not true. He wore only men's clothes from his underwear out. He favored fabrics that weren't very masculine, like silk shirts, anything with a smooth, elegant feel, but they were made strictly for men.

None of that was important now, however. Father and Marvin were living together under the same roof, and the atmosphere was becoming more unlivable with each passing day. Father was constantly on the alert, watching us next door, watching Marvin down the hall. Occasionally Marvin would crawl out of bed and go to his window, which looked out on our upstairs windows. From there he and Mother could talk. If he was in a fairly good mood, we could tease him. "How can you fly like an eagle when you're surrounded by turkeys?" we'd ask him. He knew what we meant but it didn't make any difference. Hearing our voices was enough. Nothing of importance was said, but Father took in every word and raged inwardly.

One afternoon in late March, I went over to the main house to check on Marvin. He wasn't in his room; he wasn't anywhere in the house. I looked outside, but no Marvin there, either. As I hurried back to the other house to tell Irene and Mother, a car pulled up along the curb. Marvin was inside, but I didn't recognize the driver, a young lady. "'Where have you been?" I yelled at Marvin as he was getting out of the car. He was dirty; his clothes were rumpled and soiled, and his coat was buttoned the wrong way. Marvin the meticulous. He was in such bad shape. "Where have you been?" I repeated.

Marvin didn't say anything. He just stood staring at me with limp arms and a hangdog expression.

"I found him walking along the freeway," the young lady said. "Cars were racing by. He could have gotten killed."

A freeway wasn't far from where we lived, but what was he thinking? Did he want a car to hit him? "Marvin, what were you doing?"

He shrugged his shoulders but didn't say a word.

"As soon as I got past him I looked back," the girl said. "I could tell who he was so I stopped to see if he needed help. He looked really troubled. I thought maybe his car broke down, but he said no. All he wanted was to go to Hollywood Park."

"The racetrack?" I asked.

"Uh huh," she said, "so I took him there. The place was closed down but the lot was open. I parked and let him walk around a while. That's what he wanted to do. Then he asked me to take him home."

"You found him and brought him back, that's all that matters. Thank God."

"What's wrong with him?" she asked.

"What? Oh, that," I said. "It's stress. He's been working too hard." With that I thanked the girl, grabbed Marvin, and led him back into the house. I could see Father at his upstairs window. He was following our every move.

"The next morning," Irene remembers, "I brought Marvin his breakfast. He kept saying his legs hurt so bad, his muscles hurt. He couldn't even move his legs over the side of the bed, so I let him sit up in bed to eat. Not much later, I took Mother Gay her breakfast. She had moved back into her own bedroom the night before to be near Marvin. I started to put her tray down when she said she wasn't ready to eat yet. She asked me to give her breakfast to Marvin.

"Mother's bedroom was between Marvin's and Father Gay's, and they all had connecting doors. You could walk from one bedroom to the other without going out into the hall. On that morning, the doors were all open. I could see Father Gay sitting on his bed as I tried to serve Mother. He could hear her tell me to give her breakfast to Marvin instead of him."

The following evening, which was Saturday, March 31st, I called Dave Simmons, so upset I could barely talk. I had just come from being with Marvin. He had accused me of all sorts of bad things. He hated me, he said. It was awful.

"Frankie was choking back tears when he called," Dave remembers. "When I heard the crazy, outlandish things Marvin had said to him, I knew Marvin was totally gone. If Marvin had any friend in the world, it was Frankie. His turning on Frankie like that told me we couldn't leave Marvin at home any longer. He had to have professional help, even if we had to take him away, fighting and kicking. Frankie and I made plans to get Marvin into a rehab hospital the next day."

My Brother

From outside the house there was no reason to believe that anyone famous lived there, or that anything unusual was going on inside.
It was a beautiful home, neat and clean and respectable looking, one
of many homes in a quiet residential neighborhood. But before another 24 hours would pass, the world would know who lived in that
house, and what had taken place inside. Photos of the place and its
occupants would make front-page news all over the world, and the
street and sidewalks would no longer be quiet.

17

Much has been written about Marvin's final hours. Very little has been accurate, however; I know, because I was there. I found Marvin after he had been shot.

To understand those tragic moments that led to Marvin's death, it's important to know how much Father loved Marvin. Marvin was the son who bore his name. Father gave of himself, his wisdom, to make Marvin a better person. But both Father and Marvin were stubborn and proud people. Both of them needed to feel superior. They were alike in so many ways, and it was those similarities that created enormous conflicts.

Father felt superior because he was a dedicated believer and teacher. Marvin because he knew he had talent as a singer and song-writer. Father was one of God's emissaries on earth; God's Word was Father's word. If it was written in the Bible, it was law. Marvin, on the other hand, believed his talents were God-given. In using his talents, he knew God would not misdirect him.

The clashing of similarities between Father and Marvin came to a sudden and shocking end on the morning of April 1st, 1984, the day before Marvin's forty-fifth birthday. When Irene told me she had heard shots, I thought she was joking. Many people who first heard the news on radio or television thought the same thing. After all, it was April Fool's Day. But once I heard Mother screaming next door, I knew it was no joke.

Dressed in my sweat suit and lying barefoot on the living room couch to watch a rerun of *Shane,* I ran to get my shoes, passing Irene along the way. "Your mother's at the gate crying," she said. "I'm going to see what's wrong with her." Irene remembers, "As I opened the gate that separated our two houses, Mother said 'shot' and collapsed in my arms. I thought *she* had been shot. Then Frankie came running to be with us. We calmed Mother Gay down a bit and took her to a nearby wooden bench. It was then she said, 'Marvin's been shot. Father shot Marvin.'"

Irene stayed outside with Mother while I went into the main house. I had to see if Marvin was okay and if there was anything I could do for him. It was *so* dark inside with all the blinds shut, just the way Marvin liked it. I couldn't hear anything except the rapid thumping and panic in my chest. If Marvin had been shot, I should hear him moaning, I told myself, unless…

"Call 911," I yelled out to Irene. I had left the front door open, but I didn't know if she'd heard me. I called out again, this time as loud as I could. As it turned out, a neighbor who had heard the shots had already called 911.

Why I didn't turn on a light as I made my way up the backstairs, I don't know. Maybe I figured I might see something I didn't want to see. The darkness, together with the frightening thoughts that raced through my mind, had me flashing back to Vietnam. There were sights there I never wanted to see again, but I had a sinking feeling that whatever was ahead of me now was all bad.

"Marvin," I called out, "where are you?" Nothing, no answer. I called again. Still no answer. "Father … are *you* up there?" He didn't answer either. Where was he? Did he still have the gun? Did he have it aimed at me now? Who would I find first? I wondered. I wanted to find both of them, but after what Mother had said, I knew it was more important to find Marvin.

I moved ahead, praying with each step. Where were the police? Where were the paramedics? Where was anyone?

At last I reached the second-floor landing, and the open door to Marvin's bedroom was just ahead. I moved on slowly, as if on automatic. "Oh, dear God," I prayed, "don't let it be bad, please. Let Marvin be okay, oh please, dear God."

As I stepped into Marvin's room all I could see at first was a rumpled mess of bedclothes, books, and papers. Then, on the floor, I found Marvin, crumpled at my feet next to his bed. He was looking up at me, dressed only in his maroon robe. I didn't know if he was dead or alive. "Marvin," I cried, "are you all right?" I dropped to my knees as I heard a muffled moan.

He seemed to be fairly alert. There was blood coming from his chest and small bloodstains on the rug where he was lying. I cradled him in my arms, then found the wound and pressed my thumb against it to try to stop the bleeding. "You're going to be fine," I told him. "The medics are on the way."

Outside, Irene was still with Mother. The paramedics had arrived, but they wouldn't come inside until the police got there, not with the weapon still in the house. Irene pleaded with them not to wait. "Please, please ... go inside," she begged.

"Who got shot?" one of the paramedics asked.

"Marvin Gaye," Irene answered.

"*The* Marvin Gaye?" asked another paramedic, a heavyset black man.

"Yes," she replied.

The paramedic turned away and shook his head. All he could say was, "Oh, my God."

When the police at last arrived, they held the paramedics back until Father and the gun were brought outside. Irene said she'd go into the house and get them both.

"I had to go in twice," Irene says, "once to get Father Gay, then to find the gun. I went up the front stairs, so I bypassed Frankie and Marvin, but I could hear Frankie yelling to me that he had found

Marvin. He kept asking for the paramedics and telling them to hurry. How fast they got to Marvin was now up to me, and I was hurrying the best I could.

"When I found Father Gay," Irene remembers, "he was sitting on the edge of his bed, slowly putting on his shoes. He seemed to be in a stupor, because when I asked him, 'What did you do with it? Where's the gun?' he just stared ahead, looking dazed. So I took him outside and left him with a policeman as far away from Mother Gay as possible. Then I went upstairs again to search for the gun. I found it under his pillow."

It seemed like forever until the paramedics came into the house. During the time Irene was in and out, I kept pressing on the wound and talking to Marvin, trying to comfort him. It was easier for him to listen than to talk, but he did manage to say, "I got what I wanted."

"Don't talk like that," I said. Marvin had to have been high on coke when he was shot, and I felt he was still in a state of mind where the drug was talking.

"No," he mumbled, "I couldn't do it myself, so I made him do it."

"Oh, Marvin," I cried, pressing my head against his, "it didn't have to be this way."

"It's good," Marvin said, his voice faint. "I ran my race. There's no more left in me."

I had held Marvin in my arms for 20 minutes before the paramedics came upstairs. He was still alive when they took him to California Hospital Medical Center, but barely. Seeing Marvin being carried out, Mother became hysterical. Then the police took Father away.

When I finally went back downstairs it was bedlam outside. A crowd had gathered in the street. Reporters and photographers were all over the place. Phones were ringing off the hook in both houses. I wanted to be by myself, but the wheels of what had happened were racing inside and my mind was spinning. I couldn't get Marvin's face, with his eyes staring at me when I found him, out of my head. Marvin was all I could think about. He had always been so giving and caring. He had always been there for me and Mother. I wanted to run away from the pain that filled my heart, but it was too deep. I wanted to cry, but I couldn't.

Irene called Dave Simmons. He was getting ready to go out, and he hadn't heard the news. "Please come and comfort Frankie," she said. "When I arrived the police were still there," Dave remembers. "Frankie and Irene were sitting together on a couch in the den, the room where Marvin had his piano. For some reason, nobody questioned me or said a word, so I just walked upstairs to Marvin's room. This was a crime scene, but instinctively, I started cleaning and moving stuff around. There wasn't a lot of blood, just enough to notice. I cleaned that up, threw a bunch of stuff I figured nobody needed to see into a box, and eventually took it down to the basement. Then I went back downstairs to be with Frankie and Irene. Later that day Little Richard came by, but he was without his makeup, so he was really Richard Penniman coming to pay his respects."

Marvin died that afternoon at 1:01 P.M.

By evening, the crowd outside the house had swelled with so many of Marvin's fans that cars were unable to get through. The initial frenzy had passed. Now everyone stood silently in the darkness, lighting candles and whispering prayers for Marvin.

There have been many theories about what had caused the argument between Marvin and Father that led to the shooting. Irene believes it was jealousy. "I honestly feel Father Gay was so distraught and so mad because Mother was always in Marvin's room. She did everything for Marvin—fixed his food for him, sat with him while he ate, rubbed his feet to make him feel better, read and prayed with him. Father was jealous of all the pampering and attention Marvin received from her. No one paid attention to him."

Dave Simmons believes it was Marvin's way of committing suicide. Says Dave, "Marvin was so shrewd. What better way to do it, and put it on the mind of the person most upset with you, and let him live with it for the rest of his time? That's the way Marvin's mind worked. He was a slickster—and the best friend anyone could ever have."

Mother once told me that Marvin had started the shouting and shoving match he had with Father that morning (an argument that had nothing to do with insurance papers, as some people believe). "Marvin just kept at him until the boiling point," she had said. "When he hit Father in the face, that was it."

If I am to believe Marvin's confession, I cannot doubt he had set up his own death. He had given Father the gun months earlier, supposedly to protect him from all the unknown people who were out to get him. But jealousy certainly contributed to Father's anger. During those last few weeks that led up to April 1st, Father was in a constant jealous rage. Mother's pampering had a lot to do with that, but his jealousy had started long before, with Marvin's success and his taking over the role of breadwinner. Father was a proud man.

Marvin certainly knew all the right buttons to push. He also knew it wouldn't take much, and it didn't, to get Father to pull the trigger. Pulling the trigger, I feel, was Father's last act of giving for Marvin.

Who really won their lifelong battle? Not Marvin, and certainly not Father. Once Father fired the shots, his life was all but over, too. In the end, it wasn't about winning—or superiority—at all.

18

More than ten thousand people, forming a line that stretched over a mile long, gathered to pay their last respects to Marvin at Forest Lawn Memorial Park's Chapel of the Hills in Los Angeles. For the public viewing, held during the early evening of April 4th, Marvin was dressed in the white military-style uniform he had worn during his final tour, with his head and neck cushioned with luxurious white ermine. His silver coffin, lined with white satin tufting, was banked with scores of floral tributes from family, friends, leading figures in the music industry, and fans.

The funeral service was held the next day at Forest Lawn's Hall of Liberty Chapel. A huge crowd had started gathering earlier in the day to get the best vantage points to watch the arrival of all the famous faces. Loudspeakers had been set up outside the chapel to broadcast the services to those unable to get inside. Everyone entering the chapel was handed a four-page program that looked hastily put together, typed and printed on a Xerox machine. A photo of Marvin standing in an early Frank Sinatra–like pose graced the cover.

The services began with a tape of Marvin's famous singing of the national anthem, followed by Bishop Simon Peter Rawlings, head of the House of God in Lexington, Kentucky, with a reading of the Twenty-third Psalm. Cecil Jenkins sang "The Lord's Prayer," and Peggy Williams sang "His Eye Is on the Sparrow." Then, according to the program, friends were scheduled to speak. That's when things began falling apart. What at first appeared to be a short, well-organized service rambled on for hours, with long waits between speakers and no time limits for the remembrances.

Quincy Jones has described the proceedings as "a mess," but I'm sure Marvin would have had a good time hearing everyone's kind words and often humorous anecdotes of their times together. Stevie Wonder and Little Richard sang songs for Marvin, Smokey Robinson offered a touching farewell, Marvin's band played, and Dick Gregory closed with a positive reference to Father, saying he wished Father were in the chapel too. "I'd tell him how much I love him," said Dick. All of Marvin's family members, except Father, were there, including Sweetsie and Jeanne, Anna and Marvin III, as well as Jan, Nona, and Bubby. Other attendees included Dave Simmons, Harvey Fuqua, Berry Gordy, Martha Reeves, Norm Whitfield, Brian and Eddie Holland, Reverend Shelton West, and Larkin Arnold.

Mother and I waited until the last of the crowd had filed out of the chapel to say our goodbyes to Marvin. It wasn't an easy wait for me. I couldn't imagine seeing Marvin lying so still after all we'd been through together. He had always been so full of life, and so much a part of mine. I knew I could never let go of him, and I didn't want to. But it helped to see him looking so peaceful at last. I couldn't have wanted more for him now.

I held Mother as she stood at Marvin's side for the final time, silently saying a prayer for her. She gently touched Marvin's cheek with her hand, and kissed him. Then the coffin lid was closed.

With Irene and Mother at my side, and little April in my arms, we followed Marvin's pallbearers—George Huely, Cecil Jenkins, Edward Smith, Ernest Thomas, Andre White, and Gary Woodward—as they carried his casket through the crowd still gathered outside the chapel. Midway along, Mother grabbed my hand.

Marvin was cremated the next day. His ashes were scattered over the waters of the Pacific by Anna and by Marvin's three children, from aboard a yacht.

Father was in Los Angeles County Men's Jail, awaiting his hearing in court, so he was unable to attend Marvin's funeral. It's unlikely that he would have anyway. There were fears for Father's life. All visitors attending his court appearances were searched by bailiffs with metal detectors, in an effort to ward off possibly vengeful fans. An examination to determine if Father was competent to stand trial revealed that he had a tumor the size of a quarter attached to the pituitary gland in his brain, which was successfully removed on May 17th. Following the operation, Father was judged competent to stand trial.

On June 15th, as Father's trial was under way, Mother sued for divorce, after nearly 50 years of marriage. She cited April 1st, the day of Marvin's death, as the official separation date. While she never wanted to deal with Father anymore, or see him again, she believed in her heart that he did not kill Marvin. She believed that Marvin committed suicide.

Mother returned to the Gramercy Place home only to collect her belongings. She stayed with sister Jeanne in her Hollywood apartment, vowing she would never live in the house again, calling it "a tomb," but she changed her mind once a decision on Father's future had been reached.

Father returned too, although only briefly. As Irene remembers, "After being in jail for a short time, he was out on bail and back at the house—this was before his brain operation. He stayed pretty much to himself, alone up in his room."

I had to get away. Living next door to the main house brought on nothing but bad memories, kept alive by Father's return, the hounding of the press, and the constant flow of people who stopped out in front wanting to see the place or take pictures of where Marvin was shot. It was almost impossible to go out our front door without everyone wanting to know more, know everything.

I'd never been to Scotland, never met the Duncans (Irene's family), and they'd never seen April. We were loading the car, getting ready to leave for the airport, when Father came out and said, "Do you think Marvin will be back from Belgium before you return?" He had, for the moment, blanked out everything that had happened.

We were away four months, and as Irene says, "I brought a little bit of color to the Duncans." We stayed with Irene's sister, Fiona. Her other sister, Gladys, put me in a kilt, then we all went for a walk. A man in a car saw me and drove off the street into a trash can; I'm sure I was the only black man in Scotland at the time.

Being away gave me a chance to do some singing of my own in Scotland and England, and on our return to North America, I worked at times with either Kim Weston or Martha Reeves in New York, California, and Canada. Those engagements led to a tribute to Marvin, an album called *Together—You and Me.* Rather than going back to Gramercy Place when we settled back in Los Angeles, we got an apartment in another section of the city.

During Father's trial, the police report from the morning of the shooting was read. Part of it stated that Father had stood outside the house with no remorse and threw the gun on the grass. Irene was aware that misinformation had been written into the record and wanted to correct it at the time, but I stopped her from saying anything when I came out of the house after being with Marvin. "Don't say any thing ... keep quiet," I told her, knowing she was then in the States only on a visitor's permit. I didn't want her getting in trouble or deported.

By the time Father stood in court, his charge had been reduced from first-degree murder to voluntary manslaughter, based on Father's age and physical ailments, as well as Marvin's aggressive provocation and drug-induced state. Father never denied having shot Marvin, even though he told the court he believed the gun was loaded only with "blanks or pellets." A plea of no contest was entered, and for the next six weeks, Father remained in custody awaiting his sentence, facing a maximum of 13 years in prison for voluntary manslaughter.

On November 2nd, the judge ordered Father released on a six-year suspended sentence, and five years' probation, calling the case "terribly tragic" and saying that Marvin provoked the incident. "It was all his fault," said the judge.

Father was sent to the Inglewood Retirement Home for the duration of his probation. After thanking the judge, he quietly asked to address the court. In a shaky voice, Father said, "If I could bring Marvin back, I would. I was afraid of him. I thought I was going to get hurt. I'm real sorry for everything that happened. I'm sorry ... I loved him."

In 1987, three years after Marvin died, Mother passed away due to cancer.

Following his five-year stay at the Inglewood Retirement Home, Father moved to Long Beach, where he died in 1998, at the age of eighty-four. When I heard that he was gone, I didn't want to think about his later years, only about the earlier times when me and Marvin were children. We didn't always understand Father's strict ways then, but as I looked back, I realized he was doing his best to shape our lives in a positive way. He instilled in us strong beliefs that, down the road, led to many of Marvin's conflicts. But he earned our respect, and without him, there never would have been a Marvin Gaye or his music for the world to enjoy.

Epilogue

Several years after Marvin's death, Irene and I returned to England. I was playing some shows in London, and we were in a taxi driving to our hotel when "I Heard It Through the Grapevine" came on over the cabbie's radio. It was Marvin's version.

The driver started singing along with it, and when the song ended, he told us how much he adored Marvin. Irene and I agreed, then she leaned forward and said, "That's his brother sitting next to me."

The cab driver glanced into his rearview mirror, looked away, then glanced again. "Man, it *is* you!" he gasped. He remained our personal cabbie for the remainder of our stay.

It wasn't until after Marvin's death that I finally came to realize just how much he meant to so many people, and just how deeply he has influenced American music. Barely a day goes by that I do not hear another young soul singer and think, "There's another one, another young Marvin." I'll read an interview in which the singer credits Marvin as one of his greatest influences. I'll discover Marvin's recordings and performances listed in various "Best Of" polls.

Like Frank Sinatra, Elvis Presley, and John Lennon, Marvin is still with us. The entertainment industry continues to celebrate his life and music through television tributes in America and abroad. His entire back catalog has been remastered and reissued. Radio plays his records as often today as when they were soaring up the charts.

Since the release of *The Big Chill* (1983), Marvin's voice has been heard on numerous film soundtracks, including *Mermaids* (1990), *The Walking Dead* (1995), *How Stella Got Her Groove Back* (1998), *Summer of Sam* (1999), and *High Fidelity* (2000). He has been the subject of several TV biographies, and his voice has been prominently featured in network promotions as well as on the soundtrack for the TV miniseries *The '70s* (2000); I'm sure there is more to come. [*In 2002, R&B singer Usher portrayed Marvin on an episode of the television show* American Dreams *that had Marvin appearing on a '60s segment of Dick Clark's* American Bandstand.]

Over the years Marvin has received so many posthumous awards and honors that they deserve to be noted in a special section of this book that lists the milestone events in his life. Besides his star on Hollywood's Walk of Fame, one of my favorite honors of Marvin's is one that came to him as we entered the new millennium: the *Los Angeles Times* listed Marvin's singing of the national anthem at the 1983 NBA All-Star game as one of Southern California's most remarkable vocal performances of the century. Said the *Times:* "Marvin Gaye transformed 'The Star-Spangled Banner' into a purifying anthem of sexuality." Added Earvin "Magic" Johnson: "My feelings were pride at being an American. It was something that ... I guess you had to be there ... that chill went through your body. You almost cried, it was so devastating. Everyone wanted to go over and give him 'five' for what he did. Just shake his hand. Hug him because it was so inspirational. It was unbelievable."

Other tributes have come from fellow singers and musicians, including Rod Stewart, Carlos Santana, Barry White, Brian McKnight, and Michael Bolton, who have all praised Marvin and dedicated

songs to him during various appearances. But the most unusual tribute came from Nelson Mandela, who revealed in a speech following his release from prison that listening to Marvin's *What's Going On*
album while he was incarcerated helped him keep his sanity.

Marvin's friends and contemporaries too have spoken of just
how profoundly he has touched their lives and has sparked their
own creativity with his music. And though years have passed since
we lost him, I feel he is still here, still making music that will live
forever.

Frankie Gaye

Important Events
in the Life of Marvin Gaye

1939 (April 2) Born Marvin Pentz Gay, Jr., in Washington, D.C.

1950 Made first stage appearance (at local playground theater in D.C.).

1953 Family moved from Simple City section of southwest D.C. to newly built projects in the northeast part of town.... Became member of D.C. Tones doo wop singing group.

1956 (October) Enlisted in Air Force.

1957 (June) Discharged from Air Force "under honorable conditions"... returned to D.C. and joined the Marquees doo wop group. Bo Diddley produced group's first recording, "Hey, Little School Girl."

1958 Met Harvey Fuqua, who absorbed the Marquees into his own group, the Moonglows.... Left D.C. for Chicago with the newly renamed Harvey and the Moonglows.

1960 Moved to Detroit, Michigan, with Fuqua after the two cut ties with the Moonglows.... Signed by Fuqua as an artist with Gwen Gordy's Anna label, a subsidiary of her brother Berry's Motown record label.... (December) Introduced

to Berry Gordy at Motown Christmas party.... Signed
with Tamla, an imprint of Motown label.

1961   (May) First single released on Tamla with "Let Your
Conscience Be Your Guide" on the A-side and "Never
Let You Go (Sha-Lu-Bop)" on the flip side.... (June) First
album, *The Soulful Moods of Marvin Gaye,* released on
Tamla.

1962   (October) Motown's roster of performers hit the road for
the first Motortown Revue. Two-month tour of US
opened at Howard Theater in Washington, D.C....
(December) "Stubborn Kind of Fellow" released, reaching
No. 8 on the R&B charts, and No. 46 on the pop charts.

1963   (June) Married Anna Gordy in Detroit.... (July) Became
Motown's biggest solo artist with the release of "Pride and
Joy."

1964   (April) Teamed with Kim Weston to record *Together*
album.... Received top billing in the latest Motortown
Revue.... Launched the Marvin Gaye Revue, which
opened in several US cities, from San Francisco to Detroit.... (October) Along with the Beach Boys, Chuck
Berry, the Rolling Stones, and others, appeared on TV's
TAMI Show.... (November) Traveled to England for TV
appearances to promote his records.... Cowrote "Dancing
in the Street" with William Stevenson.... Won *Detroit
Courier*'s jazz poll and Comb and Clipper contest, as top
male vocalist.

1965   (January) "How Sweet It Is (To Be Loved by You)"
reached No. 6 on the US charts.... (November) "Ain't
That Peculiar" became another million-seller as it topped
the R&B charts.

1966   (December) Recorded first single with Tammi Terrell:
"Ain't No Mountain High Enough."

1967 "Your Precious Love" duet with Tammi Terrell became pair's first Top Ten success in US…. (October) Tammi Terrell collapsed during concert at Hampden-Sydney College in Virginia.

1968 "If I Could Build My Whole World Around You" duet with Terrell hit No. 10 on US charts…. (May) "Ain't Nothing Like the Real Thing," also sung with Terrell, reached No. 8…. (September) "You're All I Need to Get By," another duet with Terrell, hit No. 7…. (October) Sang national anthem before World Series game between Detroit Tigers and St. Louis Cardinals…. (November) Had first No. 1 pop single (a chart-topper for seven weeks) with "I Heard It Through the Grapevine"; the song was also biggest-selling single in Motown's history…. (December) Performed at Miami Pop Festival with Chuck Berry, Fleetwood Mac, Junior Walker, and others.

1969 (March) "Grapevine" hit No. 1 in Great Britain and became an international sensation…. (June) Performed at the Newport '69 festival at San Fernando State College in California.

1970 (March) Tammi Terrell died.

1971 (January) "What's Going On" was released as a single, and became Motown's fastest-selling recording…. (March) Began recording *What's Going On* album, which was released in May 1971 and broke all existing sales records when a half-million copies were sold on its first day of release…. Swept the NAACP's Image Awards for Producer of the Year, Male Vocalist of the Year, and Album of the Year…. Honored by *Record World* with its awards for Record of the Year and Male Vocalist of the Year…. *Time Magazine* named *What's Going On* one of the Top Ten albums of the year, describing Marvin as "part mystic, part Pentecostal fundamentalist, part socially aware ghetto graduate"….

"Mercy Mercy Me (The Ecology)" and "Inner City Blues (Make Me Wanna Holler)" released as singles; reached No. 4 and No. 9, respectively, on the charts.

1972 (May) Marvin Gaye Day celebration in Washington, D.C.... Honored by *Billboard Magazine* with its Trendsetter Award for "promoting the cause of ecology through thought-provoking message songs."... Composed the film score for *Trouble Man* while in Hollywood.

1973 (January) Visited Jamaica for concert to benefit Boys Club of Trench Town. Received key to the city of Kingston from Jamaican Prime Minister.... Recorded songs for *Let's Get It On* album at Motown's Hitsville studio in Holly-wood. Met Janice Hunter during recording session for title song, on March 22.... When called "a dedicated re-cluse" by *Los Angeles Times,* Marvin described himself as "an underground person. That's why I don't really want any publicity. I would rather not have my thoughts spread all over the country."

1974 In Oakland, California, performed in concert for the first time in four years; the concert material became source for *Marvin Gaye Live!* album, released in August.... (October) Honored at Marvin Gaye Days in Oklahoma City.... Named Honorary Citizen of Omaha, Nebraska.

1975 (March) Received commendation from the city of Los Angeles, signed by Mayor Tom Bradley, citing "Marvin Gaye as a gifted composer and accomplished musician, a performer's performer...."

1976 (May) Honored at United Nations Headquarters, in New York City, for his contribution to the US National Commission for UNESCO, following his benefit concert at Radio City Music Hall. Proceeds from the concert were given to the Emergency Relief Fund for the National Association for the Advancement of Colored People (NAACP).... (September) Recorded majority of songs for two-LP album, *Live! At the London Palladium,* during sold-out overseas concert.... Named by US State Department as "Ambassador of Good Will," in recognition of his work on behalf of children around the world.

1977 (March) Marriage to Anna Gordy Gaye legally ended.... (October) Married Janice Hunter in New Orleans.

1978 (September) Signed seven-year contract with Motown.

1979 (January) Ranked by *Billboard Magazine* among its Top Ten performers of all time.... (February) Teamed with Stevie Wonder, Diana Ross, and Smokey Robinson for "Pops We Love You," a tribute single honoring Berry Gordy's father on his 90th birthday.... (September) Attended the Sugar Ray Leonard–Andy Price prizefight at Caesar's Palace, in Las Vegas. That same evening, sang the national anthem before a live network television audience, prior to the main-event championship fight between Larry Holmes and Ernie Shavers.... (November) Departed for concerts in Hawaii and Japan, then returned to Hawaii to begin self-imposed exile.

1980 (June) Departed Hawaii for concert tour of Great Britain, the Netherlands, and Switzerland.... (July) Tour ended in controversy after he arrived late for performance at Royal Gala Charity Show, held at Lakeside Country Club in Surrey. Princess Margaret, a fan, had departed before he arrived.

1981 (February) Left England for Belgium, with son Bubby, Bubby's nanny, and Freddy Cousaert.... Signed contract with Columbia Records, ending his long relationship with Motown.

1982   Recorded *Midnight Love* album at Studio Katy in Ohaine, Belgium.... (October) Departed Belgium for the United States, after a three-year absence.

1983   (February) Sang the national anthem at the NBA All-Star Game in Los Angeles. His version, it was noted, put the anthem "into another groove".... 25th annual Grammy awards brought Marvin two Grammys for "Sexual Healing": Best Male Vocalist and Best Instrumental Performance in R&B, at Shrine Auditorium, in Los Angeles.... (March) Joined former Motown artists for taping of 25th anniversary special at the Civic Auditorium, in Pasadena, California.... (April) Opened four-month-long final tour in San Diego, California.... (August) Gave final performance at Greek Theater in Los Angeles.

1984   (April 1) Died after being shot by his father, one day before his 45th birthday.... (April 4) Family, friends, and fans gathered at Forest Lawn Memorial Park, in Los Angeles, to pay last respects at public viewing. Private funeral held the following day.

Posthumous Honors and Awards

1985   (January) Marvin's acclaimed 1983 rendition of national anthem was the first video to be shown on new VH1 cable channel.... "Missing You," a tribute song written by Lionel Richie and sung by Diana Ross, reached No. 10 on the charts.

1987   (January) Inducted into the Rock and Roll Hall of Fame at the Waldorf Astoria Hotel, in New York City.

1988   "Peasie" Adams started Marvin Gaye Appreciation Day at Watts playground in Washington, D.C., and began crusade to have park near the Gay family row house named in his honor.... *Rolling Stone* issued its list of the 100 best singles from the past 25 years. Two Marvin Gaye singles made the Top 15: "I Heard It Through the Grapevine" (No. 4) and "What's Going On" (No. 14).

1990 (September) Star was dedicated on Hollywood Walk of Fame. Stevie Wonder and Lou Rawls were among the celebrities at ceremony.

1995 (November) Inducted into Soul Train Hall of Fame at 25th annual Soul Train Awards, at Shrine Auditorium, in Los Angeles.... the $150 million Hard Rock Hotel and Casino, in Las Vegas, opened with a special Marvin Gaye room to celebrate his career.

1996 (February) Honored with Lifetime Achievement Award, during a tribute at 38th annual Grammy awards, at Shrine Auditorium, in Los Angeles.

1998 *Los Angeles Times* readers' poll of the Top 100 pop albums of all time listed "What's Going On" at No. 11.

1999 Marvin's singing of "Sexual Healing," during the 1983 Grammy awards show, was named the No. 2 Greatest Grammy Moment of all time.

2000 "What's Going On" was included in National Public Radio's list of the 100 most important American musical works of the 20th century.

Acknowledgments

Heartfelt thanks to our publisher, Backbeat Books; our irreplaceable literary agents, Mike Hamilburg and Sherrill Chidiac; and to many of Marvin's friends, family, coworkers, and fans, who shared their memories, revived others, and responded to our calls without hesitation.

At Backbeat, we are most grateful to the following very special people for their guidance, kindness, and enthusiasm from day one: Matt Kelsey, Dorothy Cox, Richard Johnston, Nancy Tabor, Nina Lesowitz, Kevin Becketti, Amy Miller, Jacqueline Celenza, and Larissa Berry.

And, of course, our deep thanks to those who helped in so many ways to make this dream come true: Geraldine "Peasie" Adams, Ron Brewington, Richard Carbajal, Gloria Carlyle, Beatrice Carson, Chuck Edwards, Jamie Marshall, Reese Palmer, Wallace Peoples, Dave Simmons, Brian Tessier, and Kim Weston.

—Frankie Gaye, Irene Gaye, and Fred E. Basten

About the Authors

Frankie Gaye and his famous brother, Marvin, were as close as brothers could be. They looked alike; they sounded alike. They both wrote music, and they both sang. Music was their lives.

Frankie and Marvin were inseparable. They kept in touch even during those times when they could not be together. As Marvin's career escalated, Frankie worked as his brother's right-hand man, overseeing Marvin's numerous concert tours and performances, as well as many of his business interests. A gifted songwriter and singer in his own right, Frankie wrote the score for the 1979 film *Penitentiary*. His recording of "My Brother" was on the charts in Great Britain during the early 1990s.

Until his sudden and untimely death in late 2001, Frankie Gaye lived in Santa Monica, California, with his wife, Irene, and their three children: April, Fiona, and Frankie, Jr.

Fred E. Basten is the author of over 25 books, primarily on Hollywood and the entertainment industry, including *Glorious Technicolor; Max Factor's Hollywood; Steve McQueen: The Final Chapter; Life at the Marmont Fabulous; Las Vegas;* and *Hollywood Archive.* Four of his books have been the basis of television documentaries on which he has appeared and served as technical adviser.

Basten grew up in the music business. His father fronted a dance band in music-mad Chicago during the big-band era, then played for stage shows at Balaban & Katz's showcase theaters in the Loop in downtown Chicago. In college Basten sang with a swing choir that performed on Capitol Records (backing Nat "King" Cole, Dean Martin, June Christy, and others); in concert (at the Hollywood Bowl, the Mocambo, and Crescendo nightclubs); and on television (on *The Ed Sullivan Show*, *The Colgate Comedy Hour*, and with Dinah Shore, Liberace, and Johnny Carson).

Fred E. Basten lives in Santa Monica, California.

Index

Index

Index

Index